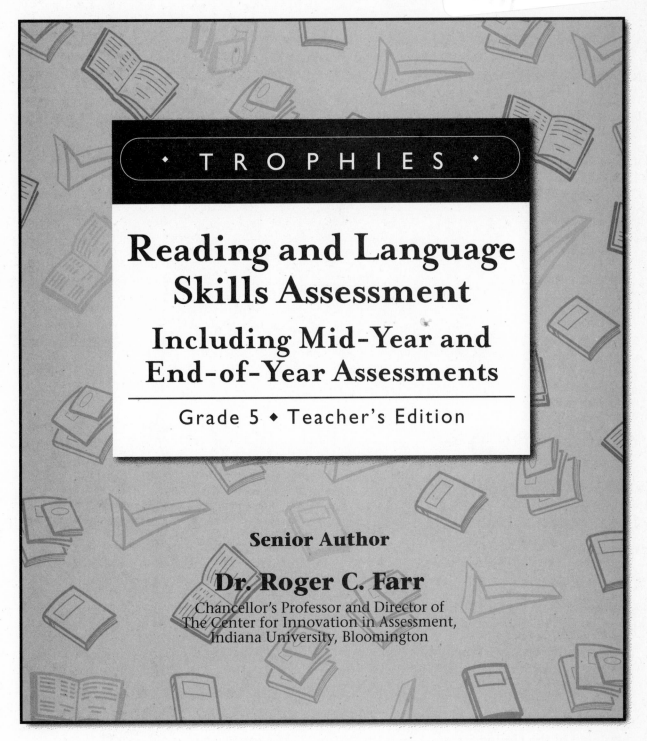

· T R O P H I E S ·

Reading and Language Skills Assessment

Including Mid-Year and End-of-Year Assessments

Grade 5 ◆ Teacher's Edition

Senior Author

Dr. Roger C. Farr

Chancellor's Professor and Director of
The Center for Innovation in Assessment,
Indiana University, Bloomington

 **Harcourt**

Orlando   Boston   Dallas   Chicago   San Diego Barbourville, KY 40906

Visit *The Learning Site!*
www.harcourtschool.com

ISBN 0-15-324965-X

9 10   170   10 09 08 07 06 05

Harcourt • Reading and Language Skills Assessment

Table of Contents

Appendix

• •

Trophies
Assessment Components

The chart below gives a brief overview of the assessment choices that are available at this grade level. The titles in boldface can be found in this Teacher's Edition.

Entry-Level Assessments	**To plan instruction**
Placement and Diagnostic Assessments	◆ To determine the best placement for a student and to diagnose strengths and weaknesses
Reading and Language Skills Pretests	◆ To determine a student's proficiency with selected skills *before* starting instruction
Formative Assessments	**To monitor student progress**
End-of-Selection Tests	◆ To monitor a student's comprehension of each selection and selection vocabulary
Oral Reading Fluency Assessment	◆ To monitor the rate and accuracy with which a student reads text aloud
Assessment notes at "point of use" in the Teacher's Edition	◆ To monitor selected skills and strategies as they are taught
Mid-Year Reading and Language Skills Assessment	◆ To monitor how well a student has retained reading and language skills
Summative Assessments	**To assess mastery of skills taught** **To assess ability to apply skills and strategies**
Reading and Language Skills Posttests	◆ To assess mastery of reading and language skills taught in a theme
Holistic Assessment	◆ To evaluate a student's ability to apply reading and writing skills and strategies to new situations
End-of-Year Reading and Language Skills Assessment	◆ To evaluate mastery of reading and language skills taught during the year

Overview of the Teacher's Edition

●●●

This Teacher's Edition is organized into two major sections. Each section contains information about a separate assessment component. The two assessment components are as follows:

Reading and Language Skills Assessments

Two parallel forms of the *Reading and Language Skills Assessments*, a Pretest and a Posttest, are available for each theme at this grade. These assessments evaluate the specific skills taught in the themes. The assessments can be used in tandem before and after instruction in the theme, or they can be used independently. For example, only the posttest could be used to evaluate how well students learned the skills taught in the theme.

Mid-Year and End-of-Year Skills Assessments

Two cumulative assessments are also included in this Teacher's Edition. The *Mid-Year Reading and Language Skills Assessment* evaluates the skills taught in the first half of the year in Themes 1 through 3. The *End-of-Year Reading and Language Skills Assessment* evaluates the skills taught during the entire year in Themes 1 through 6.

Copying masters for all of the assessment booklets are located in the Appendix. They are organized as follows:

Theme 1   *Reading and Language Skills Assessment*
Theme 2   *Reading and Language Skills Assessment*
Theme 3   *Reading and Language Skills Assessment*
Mid-Year Reading and Language Skills Assessment

Theme 4   *Reading and Language Skills Assessment*
Theme 5   *Reading and Language Skills Assessment*
Theme 6   *Reading and Language Skills Assessment*
End-of-Year Reading and Language Skills Assessment

Reading and Language Skills Assessments

Description of the Assessments

The *Reading and Language Skills Assessments* are criterion-referenced tests designed to measure students' achievement on the skills taught in each of the themes. Criterion-referenced scores help teachers make decisions regarding the type of additional instruction that students may need.

Six *Reading and Language Skills Assessments* are available at this grade level—one assessment for each theme. The assessments evaluate students' achievement in decoding, vocabulary, literary response and analysis, comprehension, research and information skills, and language. The formats used on the *Reading and Language Skills Assessments* follow the same style as those used in instruction. This ensures that the assessments are aligned with the instruction.

Scheduling the Assessments

The *Reading and Language Skills Assessments* have been designed to correlate with specific skills introduced and reinforced within each theme of the program. Therefore, a *Reading and Language Skills Assessment Pretest* could be administered before a theme is started to determine which skills need to be emphasized. Or, a *Reading and Language Skills Assessment Posttest* could be administered after a theme is completed to verify that students can apply the skills that were taught.

If possible, a *Reading and Language Skills Assessment* should be given in one session. The pace at which you administer the assessment will depend on your particular class and group. The assessments are not timed. Most students should be able to complete an assessment in thirty to forty-five minutes.

Directions for Administering

Accommodations can be made for students with special needs (e.g., special education, ELL). If accommodations are made for a student, they should be noted in the space provided on the cover of the assessment booklet.

Prior to administering a *Reading and Language Skills Assessment*, the following general directions should be read to the students.

Say: *Today you will be answering questions about some of the things we have learned together in class. Do your very best and try to answer each of the questions.*

When administering the assessment, repeat or clarify items that students do not hear or directions that they do not understand, but do not permit such explanations to reveal any answers.

The directions for each assessment are printed on the pages of the assessment booklets. There are no additional directions. If you wish, you may have students read the directions silently by themselves, or you may choose to read the directions aloud while students read them silently. Remember, if necessary, you may clarify any directions that students do not understand, as long as the clarification does not reveal any answers. Allow enough time for all students to complete the assessment or portion of the assessment being administered.

Scoring and Interpreting the Assessments

The *Reading and Language Skills Assessment* can be scored using the answer keys. Follow these steps:

1. Turn to the appropriate answer key in the Appendix.
2. Compare the student's responses, item by item, to the answer key and put a check mark next to each item that is correctly answered.
3. Count the number of correct responses for each skill or subtest and write this number on the "Pupil Score" line on the booklet cover. Add the Pupil Scores for each skill to obtain the Total Score.
4. Determine if the student met the criterion for each skill.

A student who scores at or above the criterion level for each subtest is considered competent in that skill area and is probably ready to move forward without additional practice. A column for writing comments about "Pupil Strength" has been provided on the cover of the assessment booklet.

A student who does not reach criterion level probably needs additional instruction and/or practice in that particular skill. Examine the student's scores for each subtest and decide whether you should reteach a particular skill, or move forward to the next theme.

For teachers who wish to keep a cumulative record of Pupil Scores across themes, a Student Record Form has been provided for that purpose in the Appendix.

A *Reading and Language Skills Assessment* is just one observation of a student's reading behavior. It should be combined with other evidence of a student's progress, such as the teacher's daily observations, student work samples, and individual reading conferences. The sum of all of this information, coupled with test scores, is more reliable and valid than any single piece of information.

Mid-Year and End-of-Year Reading and Language Skills Assessments

....

Description of the Assessments

The *Mid-Year* and *End-of-Year Reading and Language Skills Assessments* are criterion-referenced tests designed to measure students' achievement on the skills taught in the themes. The assessments evaluate students' achievement in decoding, vocabulary, literary response and analysis, comprehension, research and information skills, and language. The assessments are designed to give a global picture of how well students apply the skills taught in the program. They are not intended to be diagnostic tests and do not yield specific scores for each skill. However, if a student does not reach the overall criterion for the total test, it is possible to judge his or her performance on the major skill categories (e.g., decoding, vocabulary, and comprehension).

The formats used on the *Mid-Year* and *End-of-Year Reading and Language Skills Assessments* follow the same style as those used in instruction. This ensures that the assessments are aligned with the instruction.

Contents of the Assessments

The following tables list the contents of the *Mid-Year* and *End-of-Year Assessments*. The contents of the *Mid-Year Reading and Language Skills Assessment* come from the skills taught in Themes 1, 2, and 3. The contents of the *End-of-Year Reading and Language Skills Assessment* come from the skills taught in Themes 1 through 6.

Mid-Year Reading and Language Skills Assessment

Skill Category	Subcategory	Objective	Items
Vocabulary	Prefixes, Suffixes, and Roots	Use prefixes, suffixes, and roots to determine or clarify meaning	1–4
Comprehension	Draw Conclusions	Use information from a reading selection, and prior knowledge to form or support a conclusion	7, 8, 13
Comprehension	Summarize and Paraphrase	Recognize a summary and a paraphrase of a passage	9, 10
Comprehension	Text Structure: Main Idea and Details	Use text structure to identify the main idea and supporting details in a passage	5, 6, 14
Comprehension	Text Structure: Sequence	Recognize and analyze text that is presented in sequential or chronological order	11, 12
Literary Response and Analysis	Narrative Elements	Identify problem or conflict and resolution in a story	15–18
Literary Response and Analysis	Figurative Language	Identify and analyze figures of speech	19, 20
Research and Information Skills	Graphic Aids	Interpret information presented in multiple formats	21–24
Language		Display command of standard English conventions	25–36

End-of-Year Reading and Language Skills Assessment

Skill Category	Subcategory	Objective	Items
Vocabulary	Prefixes, Suffixes, and Roots	Use prefixes, suffixes, and roots to determine or clarify word meaning	1, 2
Vocabulary	Word Relationships	Understand how words are related and use context to determine word meaning	3, 4
Vocabulary	Classify/ Categorize	Classify and categorize related words	5, 6
Vocabulary	Connotation/ Denotation	Discriminate shades of meaning in related words	7, 8
Comprehension	Summarize and Paraphrase	Recognize a summary or a paraphrase of a passage	13
Comprehension	Text Structure: Main Idea and Details	Use text structure to identify the main idea and supporting details in a passage	17–19
Comprehension	Fact and Opinion	Distinguish between fact and opinion	9, 10, 12
Comprehension	Text Structure: Compare and Contrast	Recognize and analyze text presented in a compare/contrast format	14–16
Comprehension	Author's Purpose and Perspective	Recognize an author's purpose and perspective	11, 20
Comprehension	Text Structure: Cause and Effect	Analyze cause-and-effect relationships in text	21, 22
Literary Response and Analysis	Characterization	Understand an author's development of characters in a story	23–26
Research and Information Skills	References and Resources	Locate information in reference sources	27–30
Language		Display command of standard English conventions	31–40

Scheduling the Assessments

The *Mid-Year* and *End-of-Year Reading and Language Skills Assessments* have been designed to correlate with specific skills introduced and reinforced within each theme of the program. Each major reading skill taught in the program is represented on the assessments. The *Mid-Year* and *End-of-Year Reading Skills Assessments* are summative tests. That is, they are designed to evaluate whether students can apply the skills learned.

The *Mid-Year Reading and Language Skills Assessment* may be given after a student has completed the first three themes of instruction at this grade level. The *End-of-Year Reading and Language Skills Assessment* may be given after a student has completed the last three themes of instruction or the entire book.

The *Mid-Year* and *End-of-Year Reading and Language Skills Assessments* should be given in one session, if possible. The pace at which you administer the assessments will depend on your particular class and group. The assessments are not timed. Most students should be able to complete each assessment in approximately forty-five minutes to an hour.

Directions for Administering

Prior to administering the *Mid-Year* and *End-of-Year Reading and Language Skills Assessments*, the following general directions should be read to the students.

Say: *Today you will be answering questions about some of the things we have learned together in class. Do your very best and try to answer each of the questions.*

Distribute the assessment booklets and have students write their names on the Name line. Then have students fold the assessment booklet so that only the page they are working on is facing up. Make sure that every student understands what to do and how to mark the answers. When testing is completed, collect the assessment booklets.

The directions for each assessment are printed on the pages of the pupil booklets. There are no additional directions. If you wish, you may have students read the directions silently by themselves, or you may choose to read the directions aloud while students read them silently. If necessary, you may clarify any directions that students do not understand, as long as the clarification does not reveal any answers. Allow enough time for all students to complete the assessment.

Teacher's Edition

Scoring and Interpreting the Assessments

The *Mid-Year* and *End-of-Year Reading Skills Assessments* can be scored by using the answer keys found in the Appendix. Follow these steps:

1. Turn to the appropriate answer key in the Appendix.

2. Compare the student's responses, item by item, to the answer key and put a check mark next to each item that is correctly answered.

3. Count the number of correct responses for each skill category and write that number on the "Pupil Score" line on the cover of the assessment booklet. Add the Pupil Scores for each skill category to obtain the student's Total Score.

4. Next, determine if the student met the criterion for Total Score. The criterion score can be found on the cover page of the assessment booklet. Use the "Interpreting Performance" chart found in this section of the Teacher's Edition booklet to interpret the student's score.

5. If a student does not reach the overall criterion on the total test, you may evaluate the student's performance on particular skill categories. Look at each skill category and determine if the student met the criterion for that skill category. Then determine the student's strengths and weaknesses for particular skill categories. Write comments in the space provided.

There are 36 items on the *Mid-Year Reading and Language Skills Assessment* and 40 on the *End-of-Year Reading and Language Skills Assessment*. For each item, a correct answer should be given 1 point, and an incorrect or missing answer should be given 0 points. Thus, a perfect score on the mid-year assessment would be 36, and a perfect score on the end-of-year assessment would be 40. Use the following performance chart to interpret score ranges.

Interpreting Performance on the
Mid-Year and *End-of-Year Reading Skills Assessments*

Total Score	Interpretation	Teaching Suggestions
Mid-Year: 26–36 **End-of-Year: 29–40**	Average to excellent understanding and use of the major reading and language skills	Students scoring at the high end of this range exceed the criterion and should have no difficulty moving forward to the next level of the program. Students scoring at the low end of this range meet the criterion and are performing at an acceptable level.
Mid-Year: 0–25 **End-of-Year: 0–28**	Fair to limited understanding and use of the major reading and language skills	Students scoring at the high end of this range are performing slightly below the criterion and may need extra help before or after moving to the next level of the program. Note whether performance varied across the skill categories tested. Examine other samples of the students' work and/or administer some of the individual assessments (e.g., Phonics Inventory, Oral Reading Fluency Assessment) to confirm their progress and pinpoint instructional needs. Students scoring at the low end of this range do not meet criterion and should have their performance verified through other measures such as some of the individual assessments available in this program, or daily work samples. Identify what specific instructional needs must be met by reviewing the student's performance on each skill category.

Teacher's Edition

A student who does not reach the criterion level may not do so for a variety of reasons. Use the questions that follow to better understand why a student may not have reached the criterion.

- *Has the student completed all parts of the program being tested on the assessment?*

If not, the results may not be valid, since the *Mid-Year Reading and Language Skills Assessment* evaluates all the major skills taught in the first three themes at this grade level, and the *End-of-Year Reading and Language Skills Assessment* evaluates all the major skills taught in Themes 1-6 at this grade level. It would be unfair to expect a student to demonstrate mastery of skills for which he or she has not received instruction.

- *Was the student having a bad day when he or she took the assessment?*

Students can experience social or emotional problems that may affect concentration and influence performance. Sometimes a problem at home or a conflict on the school playground carries over into the classroom and interferes with performance. Recall any unusual behavior you observed before or during the testing, or confer with the student to identify any factors that may have adversely affected performance. If the student's limited performance can be attributed to extraneous problems, readminister the assessment under better conditions or discard the results.

- *Does the student perform differently on group tests than on individual tests?*

Student performance can fluctuate depending on the context and mode of the assessment. Some students perform better in a one-on-one setting that fosters individual attention than they do in a group setting that is less personal. Others are more successful reading orally than reading silently. Likewise, some students feel more comfortable answering open-ended questions orally than they do answering multiple-choice questions on a paper-and-pencil test.

- *Does the student perform differently on tests than on daily activities?*

Compare the student's performance on the mid-year and the end-of-year assessment with his or her performance on other formal types of assessment, such as theme tests and standardized tests. Also note how the student's performance compares with his or her performance on informal types of assessment, such as portfolios, reading logs, and anecdotal observation records. If the results are similar, it would suggest that the mid-year and the end-of-year results are valid and accurately represent the student's performance. If the results are not consistent, explore alternative explanations.

To resolve conflicts regarding the student's performance, you may want to collect additional evidence. For example, you may want to administer some of the individual assessments available with this program (e.g., Phonics Inventory, Oral Reading Fluency Assessment).

As with all assessments, it is important not to place too much faith in a single test. The *Mid-Year and End-of-Year Reading and Language Skills Assessments* are just one observation of a student's reading behavior. They should be combined with other evidence of a student's progress, such as the teacher's daily observations, the student's work samples, and individual reading conferences. The sum of all this information, combined with test scores, is more reliable and valid than any single piece of information.

Appendix

• •

Answer Keys for *Reading and Language Skills Assessments:*
Pretests and Posttests
Distant Voyages/Theme 1

PRETEST	POSTTEST
VOCABULARY:	**VOCABULARY:**
Prefixes, Suffixes, Roots	**Prefixes, Suffixes, Roots**
1. C	1. A
2. D	2. C
3. B	3. D
4. C	4. C
5. B	5. A
6. A	6. B
7. B	7. C
8. C	8. A
LITERARY RESPONSE AND ANALYSIS:	**LITERARY RESPONSE AND ANALYSIS:**
Narrative Elements	**Narrative Elements**
9. B	9. C
10. C	10. B
11. A	11. C
12. D	12. D
LANGUAGE	**LANGUAGE**
13. C	13. B
14. C	14. A
15. A	15. D
16. B	16. B
17. A	17. A
18. B	18. C
19. C	19. B
20. D	20. C
21. D	21. D
22. B	22. A

PRETEST	POSTTEST
COMPREHENSION: **Draw Conclusions** 1. C 2. A 3. B 4. D	**COMPREHENSION:** **Draw Conclusions** 1. C 2. B 3. A 4. D
COMPREHENSION: **Summarize and Paraphrase** 5. A 6. B 7. C 8. A	**COMPREHENSION:** **Summarize and Paraphrase** 5. C 6. D 7. A 8. B
LITERARY RESPONSE **AND ANALYSIS:** **Figurative Language** 9. D 10. B 11. D 12. A	**LITERARY RESPONSE** **AND ANALYSIS:** **Figurative Language** 9. C 10. D 11. B 12. A
LANGUAGE 13. D 14. B 15. C 16. B 17. A 18. C 19. A 20. B 21. C 22. D	**LANGUAGE** 13. B 14. D 15. A 16. D 17. B 18. A 19. D 20. C 21. A 22. D

Answer Keys for *Reading and Language Skills Assessments: Pretests and Posttests*
Distant Voyages/Theme 3

PRETEST	POSTTEST
COMPREHENSION: **Text Structure: Main Idea and Details**	**COMPREHENSION:** **Text Structure: Main Idea and Details**
1. B	1. A
2. D	2. B
3. A	3. D
4. A	4. B
COMPREHENSION: **Text Structure: Sequence**	**COMPREHENSION:** **Text Structure: Sequence**
5. B	5. D
6. D	6. C
7. A	7. B
8. B	8. A
RESEARCH AND INFORMATION SKILLS: **Graphic Aids**	**RESEARCH AND INFORMATION SKILLS:** **Graphic Aids**
9. D	9. A
10. B	10. D
11. C	11. D
12. D	12. C
LANGUAGE	**LANGUAGE**
13. C	13. B
14. D	14. C
15. A	15. A
16. B	16. B
17. D	17. C
18. B	18. A
19. A	19. B
20. B	20. A
21. C	21. C
22. A	22. D

Answer Keys for *Reading and Language Skills Assessments:*
Pretests and Posttests
*Distant Voyages/*Theme 4

PRETEST	POSTTEST
VOCABULARY: **Word Relationships**	**VOCABULARY:** **Word Relationships**
1. B	1. D
2. C	2. B
3. D	3. B
4. A	4. A
VOCABULARY: **Classify/Categorize**	**VOCABULARY:** **Classify/Categorize**
5. A	5. C
6. C	6. B
7. D	7. A
8. C	8. B
COMPREHENSION: **Fact and Opinion**	**COMPREHENSION:** **Fact and Opinion**
9. C	9. B
10. D	10. D
11. D	11. A
12. B	12. C
LANGUAGE	**LANGUAGE**
13. C	13. B
14. D	14. A
15. A	15. B
16. C	16. C
17. A	17. C
18. A	18. B
19. B	19. B
20. C	20. A
21. B	21. D
22. D	22. C

PRETEST	POSTTEST
COMPREHENSION: **Text Structure: Compare and Contrast**	**COMPREHENSION:** **Text Structure: Compare and Contrast**
1. A	1. C
2. C	2. C
3. D	3. A
4. B	4. B
COMPREHENSION: **Author's Purpose and Perspective**	**COMPREHENSION:** **Author's Purpose and Perspective**
5. B	5. A
6. A	6. A
7. C	7. B
8. C	8. D
LITERARY RESPONSE AND ANALYSIS: Characterization	**LITERARY RESPONSE AND ANALYSIS: Characterization**
9. C	9. B
10. B	10. C
11. A	11. A
12. C	12. D
LANGUAGE	**LANGUAGE**
13. C	13. A
14. A	14. A
15. C	15. B
16. B	16. D
17. B	17. C
18. A	18. D
19. D	19. B
20. B	20. A
21. D	21. C
22. B	22. D

PRETEST	POSTTEST
VOCABULARY AND CONCEPTS: **Connotation/Denotation**	**VOCABULARY AND CONCEPTS:** **Connotation/Denotation**
1. D	1. B
2. B	2. D
3. C	3. A
4. D	4. C
COMPREHENSION: **Text Structure: Cause and Effect**	**COMPREHENSION:** **Text Structure: Cause and Effect**
5. C	5. B
6. A	6. A
7. B	7. B
8. B	8. C
RESEARCH AND INFORMATION SKILLS: **References and Resources**	**RESEARCH AND INFORMATION SKILLS:** **References and Resources**
9. C	9. A
10. B	10. C
11. A	11. B
12. D	12. B
LANGUAGE	**LANGUAGE**
13. A	13. B
14. C	14. A
15. D	15. B
16. C	16. D
17. B	17. D
18. C	18. B
19. C	19. C
20. A	20. B
21. C	21. D
22. B	22. D

Answer Key
Mid-Year Reading and Language Skills Assessment

VOCABULARY
1. B
2. C
3. A
4. A

COMPREHENSION
5. D
6. D
7. B
8. B
9. D
10. C
11. C
12. A
13. B
14. B

LITERARY RESPONSE AND ANALYSIS
15. D
16. C
17. A
18. B
19. B
20. A

RESEARCH AND INFORMATION SKILLS
21. B
22. A
23. C
24. C

LANGUAGE
25. D
26. C
27. A
28. A
29. C
30. B
31. C
32. D
33. B
34. A
35. A
36. C

Answer Key

End-of-Year Reading and Language Skills Assessment

VOCABULARY	LITERARY RESPONSE AND ANALYSIS
1. B	23. B
2. B	24. A
3. C	25. C
4. A	26. D
5. D	
6. A	
7. C	
8. B	**RESEARCH AND INFORMATION SKILLS**
	27. D
COMPREHENSION	28. A
9. B	29. C
10. D	30. B
11. B	
12. C	
13. A	**LANGUAGE**
14. A	31. C
15. C	32. D
16. B	33. A
17. B	34. B
18. D	35. B
19. C	36. D
20. A	37. A
21. B	38. C
22. A	39. B
	40. A

Student Record Form
Reading and Language Skills Assessment
Trophies
Grade 5

Name _____ **Grade** _____

Teacher _____

	CRITERION SCORE	PUPIL SCORE	COMMENTS
Theme 1			
Prefixes, suffixes, and roots	6/8	___/8	_____
Narrative elements	3/4	___/4	_____
Language	7/10	___/10	_____
Theme 2			
Draw conclusions	3/4	___/4	_____
Summarize and paraphrase	3/4	___/4	_____
Figurative language	3/4	___/4	_____
Language	7/10	___/10	_____
Theme 3			
Text Structure: main idea and details	3/4	___/4	_____
Text Structure: sequence	3/4	___/4	_____
Graphic aids	3/4	___/4	_____
Language	7/10	___/10	_____

Teacher's Edition

Name _____ **Grade** _____

Teacher _____

	CRITERION SCORE	PUPIL SCORE	COMMENTS
Theme 4			
Word relationships	3/4	___/4	_____
Classify/Categorize	3/4	___/4	_____
Fact and opinion	3/4	___/4	_____
Language	7/10	___/10	_____
Theme 5			
Text Structure: compare and contrast	3/4	___/4	_____
Author's purpose and perspective	3/4	___/4	_____
Characterization	3/4	___/4	_____
Language	7/10	___/10	_____
Theme 6			
Connotation/Denotation	3/4	___/4	_____
Text Structure: cause and effect	3/4	___/4	_____
References and resources	3/4	___/4	_____
Language	7/10	___/10	_____

· T R O P H I E S ·

Reading and Language Skills Assessment Pretest

Distant Voyages/Theme 1

Name _____ Date _____

SKILL AREA	Criterion Score	Pupil Score	Pupil Strength
VOCABULARY			
Prefixes, Suffixes, Roots	6/8	_____	_____
LITERARY RESPONSE AND ANALYSIS			
Narrative Elements	3/4	_____	_____
LANGUAGE	7/10	_____	_____
Declarative and Interrogative Sentences			
Imperative and Exclamatory Sentences			
Complete and Simple Subjects			
Complete and Simple Predicates			
Compound Subjects and Predicates			
TOTAL SCORE	16/22	_____	_____

Were accommodations made in administering this test? ☐ Yes ☐ No

Type of accommodations: _____

_____

VOCABULARY: Prefixes, Suffixes, Roots

Directions: Read each sentence. Fill in the answer circle in front of the correct answer for each question.

1. **Frederick Douglass was a strong antislavery supporter.**
   What does the word *antislavery* mean?
   Ⓐ before slavery
   Ⓑ slavery again
   Ⓒ against slavery
   Ⓓ half slavery

2. Which prefix should be added to the word *workers* to make it mean "those who work together"?
   Ⓐ *sub-*
   Ⓑ *multi-*
   Ⓒ *in-*
   Ⓓ *co-*

3. Which prefix should be added to the word *print* to make it mean "print into"?
   Ⓐ *de-*
   Ⓑ *im-*
   Ⓒ *co-*
   Ⓓ *anti-*

4. **The governor called for the creation of a special committee.**
   What does the word *creation* mean?
   Ⓐ able to create
   Ⓑ one who creates
   Ⓒ act of creating
   Ⓓ without creating

GO ON

VOCABULARY: Prefixes, Suffixes, Roots (continued)

5. **The crowd at the circus reacted with astonishment as the acrobats performed.**

   What does the word *astonishment* mean?

   (A) one who astonishes

   (B) an astonished state

   (C) able to be astonished

   (D) not astonished

6. Which suffix should be added to the word *courage* to make it mean "having courage"?

   (A) *-ous*

   (B) *-ly*

   (C) *-able*

   (D) *-est*

7. Which word has the same root word as *transport* and *portable*?

   (A) transfer

   (B) porter

   (C) translation

   (D) portrait

8. Which root word means *heat*?

   (A) "ped" as in **pedal**

   (B) "manu" as in **manuscript**

   (C) "therm" as in **thermostat**

   (D) "aster" as in **asteroid**

Harcourt • Reading and Language Skills Assessment

LITERARY RESPONSE AND ANALYSIS: Narrative Elements

Directions: Read the passage. Fill in the answer circle in front of the correct answer for each question.

Miriam was worried. Her report on Egypt was due tomorrow, and she was stuck. The electricity was out all over town. The library had closed early. She couldn't even use her computer because there was no electricity in her house.

"Mr. Lyons will probably understand and give everyone an extra day," Miriam told herself. But she did not feel better. Mr. Lyons could be pretty strict. He might say, "You should have planned ahead." Miriam did not want to take the chance, but how could she get the information and pictures she needed? Maybe her brother would drive her to Haysville. The power was probably on there, and the library would be open. But Haysville was almost an hour away. Would there be time?

She knocked on Richard's door. He let her in, and she explained her problem. When she finished, Richard smiled and said, "I have a much easier solution. My laptop computer has a battery that will run for three hours. You can use the on line encyclopedia to do research, and then you can type your report. You can even download pictures and put them into your report. The only thing you won't be able to do is print the report. You'll have to hope that the power is back on by morning."

Miriam did everything her brother suggested. When she woke up, she smiled because she heard Mr. Healy using his electric hedge clippers outside.

9. The main character in this story is _____.
   (A) Richard
   (B) Miriam
   (C) Mr. Lyons
   (D) Mr. Healy

10. The problem in this story is best described as _____.
   (A) a family argument
   (B) a misunderstanding
   (C) an approaching deadline
   (D) a rivalry between two cities

GO ON

LITERARY RESPONSE AND ANALYSIS: Narrative Elements (continued)

11. The problem is caused by a _____.

Ⓐ power failure

Ⓑ computer error

Ⓒ stubborn person

Ⓓ lazy person

12. How does Miriam know that the problem will be resolved?

Ⓐ School will be closed because the power is still out.

Ⓑ The weather must be nice because Mr. Healy is working outdoors.

Ⓒ The library in Haysville has many books about Egypt.

Ⓓ The power must be back on because Mr. Healy is using electric clippers.

STOP

Score _____

Distant Voyages / Theme 1

Harcourt • Reading and Language Skills Assessment

LANGUAGE

Directions: Choose the best answer for each question.

13. Which group of words is a **sentence**?

Ⓐ Moved slowly up the steep slope.

Ⓑ The old, enormous sea turtle.

Ⓒ Waves gently lapped against the shore.

Ⓓ Slept soundly in its underground burrow.

14. What **kind of sentence** is this?
Always apply sunscreen before going swimming.

Ⓐ declarative

Ⓑ interrogative

Ⓒ imperative

Ⓓ exclamatory

15. Which sentence has the correct **end punctuation**?

Ⓐ Did you enjoy the school talent show?

Ⓑ Wow, this is the prettiest sunset I've ever seen.

Ⓒ The spotlights shone on the stage!

Ⓓ The eagle's talons are as sharp as knives?

GO ON

LANGUAGE (continued)

Directions: Read each sentence. Choose the underlined noun that is the **simple subject** of each sentence.

16. During the 1800s, many pioneers in Kentucky lived in log cabins.
    (A) 1800s
    (B) pioneers
    (C) Kentucky
    (D) cabins

17. Life on the western frontier required strength and courage.
    (A) Life
    (B) frontier
    (C) strength
    (D) courage

18. After the Civil War, government leaders made plans to reunite the nation.
    (A) Civil War
    (B) leaders
    (C) plans
    (D) nation

GO ON

Distant Voyages / Theme 1

Harcourt • Reading and Language Skills Assessment

LANGUAGE (continued)

> **Directions:** Read each sentence. Choose the underlined word that is the **simple predicate,** or verb, in each sentence.
>
> **19.** A <u>major</u> oil <u>spill</u> <u>polluted</u> the <u>coast</u> of Alaska.
>   - Ⓐ major
>   - Ⓑ spill
>   - Ⓒ polluted
>   - Ⓓ coast
>
> **20.** The <u>hind</u> <u>flippers</u> of <u>sea</u> lions <u>fold</u> under their bodies.
>   - Ⓐ hind
>   - Ⓑ flippers
>   - Ⓒ sea
>   - Ⓓ fold
>
>
>
> **Directions:** Read each pair or group of sentences. Choose the answer that shows the best way to combine the sentences.
>
> **21.** We carefully studied the directions. We assembled the model car.
>   - Ⓐ We carefully studied; we carefully assembled the model car.
>   - Ⓑ We studied the model and assembled the model carefully.
>   - Ⓒ We studied and assembled carefully, the model car.
>   - Ⓓ We carefully studied the directions and assembled the model car.
>
> **22.** Milk is a good source of protein. Fish is a good source of protein. Lean meat is a good source of protein.
>   - Ⓐ Milk and fish and lean meat are protein and sources.
>   - Ⓑ Milk, fish, and lean meat are good sources of protein.
>   - Ⓒ Milk, fish and lean meat are sources, are sources of protein.
>   - Ⓓ Milk is good, fish is good, lean meat is good, sources of protein.

STOP

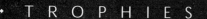

Look Inside / Theme 1

Reading and Language Skills Assessment

Harcourt

Orlando   Boston   Dallas   Chicago   San Diego

Part No. 9997-37762-1

ISBN 0-15-332204-7 (Package of 12)

5

TROPHIES

Reading and Language Skills
Assessment Posttest

Distant Voyages/Theme 1

Name _____ Date _____

SKILL AREA	Criterion Score	Pupil Score	Pupil Strength
VOCABULARY Prefixes, Suffixes, Roots	6/8	_____	_____
LITERARY RESPONSE AND ANALYSIS Narrative Elements	3/4	_____	_____
LANGUAGE Declarative and Interrogative Sentences Imperative and Exclamatory Sentences Complete and Simple Subjects Complete and Simple Predicates Compound Subjects and Predicates	7/10	_____	_____
TOTAL SCORE	16/22	_____	_____

Were accommodations made in administering this test? ☐ Yes ☐ No

Type of accommodations: _____

_____

Harcourt • Reading and Language Skills Assessment

VOCABULARY: Prefixes, Suffixes, Roots

Directions: Read each sentence. Fill in the answer circle in front of the correct answer for each question.

1. **The store owners had an inflow of business when they lowered their prices.**
   What does the word *inflow* mean?
   - (A) a flowing into
   - (B) a flowing against
   - (C) a flowing across
   - (D) a flowing out

2. Which prefix should be added to the word *classified* to make it mean "the opposite of classified"?
   - (A) *co-*
   - (B) *pre-*
   - (C) *de-*
   - (D) *over-*

3. Which prefix should be added to the word *surface* to make it mean "under the surface"?
   - (A) *multi-*
   - (B) *mid-*
   - (C) *mis-*
   - (D) *sub-*

4. **The encouragement of my parents allowed me to succeed.**
   What does the word *encouragement* mean?
   - (A) one who encourages
   - (B) without encouraging
   - (C) act of encouraging
   - (D) not encouraging

GO ON

VOCABULARY: Prefixes, Suffixes, Roots (continued)

5. **The singers gave a joyous performance.**
   What does the word *joyous* mean?
   (A) full of joy
   (B) without joy
   (C) lacking joy
   (D) resembling joy

6. Which suffix should be added to the word *graduate* to make it mean "the process of graduating"?
   (A) *-ly*
   (B) *-ion*
   (C) *-er*
   (D) *-able*

7. Which root word means *carry*?
   (A) "sign" as in **signal**
   (B) "aud" as in **audible**
   (C) "port" as in **import**
   (D) "man" as in **manual**

8. **The neighbor's loud vocalizing was disturbing us.**
   What part of the word *vocalizing* means "voice"?
   (A) voc
   (B) ali
   (C) zing
   (D) cal

Score _____

STOP

LITERARY RESPONSE AND ANALYSIS: Narrative Elements

Directions: Read the passage. Fill in the answer circle in front of the correct answer for each question.

The spelling bee had come to the final round. Only Roger Schwartz and Tina Martinez remained. It was Tina's turn. Mr. Gould, the judge, took the next card from his assistant and announced Tina's word. "Accommodate," he said.

Tina knew this one. "Two C's and two M's," she recalled. "A-C-C-O-M-M-O-D-A-T-E," she answered confidently.

Roger's word was "aquarium." He knew it did not have two C's, but he couldn't remember clearly whether it had one C. "A-C-Q-U-A-R-I-U-M," he thought to himself. That didn't seem correct. He tried to picture the way it looked written out on the fish tank at the downtown museum. His time was nearly up. He spelled it the other way, "A-Q-U-A-R-I-U-M."

"Correct," Mr. Gould said. "We'll go to another round."

Roger's mother and father smiled encouragingly at him.

Tina's mother and father gave her nods of approval.

9. The main characters in this story are _____.
   Ⓐ Mr. and Mrs. Schwartz
   Ⓑ Mr. and Mrs. Martinez
   Ⓒ Tina and Roger
   Ⓓ Mr. Gould and his assistant

10. The conflict in this story is best described as a _____.
    Ⓐ social protest
    Ⓑ school contest
    Ⓒ personal feud
    Ⓓ family argument

11. Both characters handle their problems similarly by thinking about_____.
    Ⓐ a fish tank
    Ⓑ a museum
    Ⓒ letters
    Ⓓ their parents

GO ON

LITERARY RESPONSE AND ANALYSIS: Narrative Elements (continued)

12. How is the conflict in this story resolved?

Ⓐ Roger comes out the winner.

Ⓑ Tina comes out the winner.

Ⓒ The game ends in a tie.

Ⓓ You cannot tell because the game has not ended.

Score _____

STOP

Harcourt • Reading and Language Skills Assessment

LANGUAGE

Directions: Choose the best answer for each question.

13. Which group of words is a **sentence**?
- (A) Is covered with thin, moist skin.
- (B) The startled deer bounded from sight.
- (C) A glistening blanket of pure white snow.
- (D) Gladly accepted the food that was offered.

14. What **kind of sentence** is this?
A pelican has a large pouch that hangs down from its bill.
- (A) declarative
- (B) interrogative
- (C) imperative
- (D) exclamatory

15. Which sentence has the correct **end punctuation**?
- (A) Prairie dogs live in underground tunnels!
- (B) Take an umbrella in case it rains?
- (C) Did your grandmother make the quilt.
- (D) Your new sports car is so beautiful!

GO ON

LANGUAGE (continued)

Directions: Read each sentence. Choose the underlined noun that is the **simple subject** of each sentence.

16. At the last <u>minute</u>, the <u>player</u> kicked the <u>football</u> over the <u>goalpost</u>.
  - Ⓐ minute
  - Ⓑ player
  - Ⓒ football
  - Ⓓ goalpost

17. Regular <u>exercise</u> keeps your <u>muscles</u> toned and strengthens your <u>heart</u> and <u>lungs</u>.
  - Ⓐ exercise
  - Ⓑ muscles
  - Ⓒ heart
  - Ⓓ lungs

18. At the <u>sound</u> of the starting <u>gun</u>, the <u>runners</u> raced down the <u>track</u>.
  - Ⓐ sound
  - Ⓑ gun
  - Ⓒ runners
  - Ⓓ track

LANGUAGE (continued)

Directions: Read each sentence. Choose the underlined word that is the **simple predicate**, or verb, in each sentence.

19. In 1876, Alexander G. Bell relayed the first telephone message.
    Ⓐ 1876
    Ⓑ relayed
    Ⓒ telephone
    Ⓓ message

20. European settlers first brought coins and paper money to North America.
    Ⓐ European
    Ⓑ first
    Ⓒ brought
    Ⓓ money

GO ON

LANGUAGE (continued)

Directions: Read each pair or group of sentences. Choose the answer that shows the best way to combine the sentences.

21. Children enjoy comic books. Adults enjoy comic books.
    Ⓐ Children, and adults enjoy books, comic books.
    Ⓑ Children and adults enjoy books, they enjoy comic books.
    Ⓒ Children enjoy and adults enjoy, comic books.
    Ⓓ Children and adults enjoy comic books.

22. Dad went to the hardware store. He bought lumber. He replaced the rotten boards in our shed.
    Ⓐ Dad went to the hardware store, bought lumber, and replaced the rotten boards in our shed.
    Ⓑ He went to the hardware store, and Dad bought timber, and Dad replaced the rotten boards in our shed.
    Ⓒ Dad and he went to the hardware store, bought and replaced rotten boards in our shed.
    Ⓓ He replaced boards in our shed, and he bought rotten lumber and he went to the hardware store.

Score _____   **STOP**

Harcourt • Reading and Language Skills Assessment

· T R O P H I E S ·

Look Inside / Theme 1
Reading and Language Skills Assessment

Harcourt

Orlando   Boston   Dallas   Chicago   San Diego

Part No. 9997-37756-7

ISBN 0-15-332204-7 (Package of 12)

TROPHIES

Reading and Language Skills
Assessment Pretest

Distant Voyages/Theme 2

Name _____ Date _____

SKILL AREA	Criterion Score	Pupil Score	Pupil Strength
COMPREHENSION			
Draw Conclusions	3/4	_____	_____
Summarize and Paraphrase	3/4	_____	_____
LITERARY RESPONSE AND ANALYSIS			
Figurative Language	3/4	_____	_____
LANGUAGE	7/10	_____	_____
Simple and Compound Sentences			
Clauses			
Complex Sentences			
Common and Proper Nouns; Abbreviations			
Singular and Plural Nouns		_____	_____
TOTAL SCORE	16/22		

Were accommodations made in administering this test? ☐ Yes ☐ No

Type of accommodations: _____

_____

Printed in the United States of America

ISBN 0-15-332204-7

9 10 170 10 09 08 07 06 05

COMPREHENSION: Draw Conclusions

Directions: Read each passage. Fill in the answer circle in front of the correct answer for each question.

The killer whale is actually a dolphin and is the largest member of that group. It is easy to identify a killer whale by its large size and its black and white color.

Killer whales hunt in packs and eat fish, sea lions, dolphins, and whales. They were given their name because they were thought to eat people. However, there is no record of a human ever being attacked and killed by a killer whale. In fact, scientists have found that killer whales can be very gentle.

Killer whales are mammals, not fish. Thus, they have lungs and breathe air. After inhaling, they hold their breath while they dive beneath the water's surface.

Killer whales are very curious and will come quite close to small boats. They have been kept in captivity and have been trained to perform for audiences.

1. Because a killer whale is a mammal, it must come to the water's surface every few minutes to _____.
   Ⓐ look for land
   Ⓑ feel the sun
   Ⓒ breathe in air
   Ⓓ search for food

2. Based on this passage, you could conclude that killer whales _____.
   Ⓐ do not deserve their name
   Ⓑ have limited intelligence
   Ⓒ are mean and vicious
   Ⓓ prefer to hunt alone

GO ON

COMPREHENSION: Draw Conclusions (continued)

Shawn checked his equipment again. He had put air in his tires that morning, but he brought his pump along anyway. Nancy or Marcus would probably need to use it. The pump rested in a holder on the frame of Shawn's bike.

Another built-in holder held Shawn's water bottle. It was full, but Shawn had a second full bottle at the bottom of his backpack in case someone else was thirsty. The backpack also held an extra inner tube, a tire patching kit, and a few simple tools.

Shawn had five one-dollar bills in his wallet in case of an emergency. Even though this trip was only ten miles and would last just about an hour, Shawn wasn't one to take chances. He adjusted the chin strap on his helmet one more time, and he pedaled off along the bike path to meet the others.

3. Based on this passage, you can conclude that Shawn tries to be _____.
   (A) well-liked
   (B) prepared
   (C) loyal
   (D) informed

4. According to the passage, Shawn probably knows how to _____.
   (A) survive without water
   (B) treat an injury
   (C) do bike tricks
   (D) fix a flat tire

STOP

Score _____   *Distant Voyages / Theme 2*

Harcourt • Reading and Language Skills Assessment

COMPREHENSION: Summarize and Paraphrase

Directions: Read each passage. Fill in the answer circle in front of the correct answer for each question.

Gwen stood before a packed auditorium, accepting an award for her impressive accomplishments. By trying again and again, working long hours, and continuing despite setbacks, Gwen had created a vaccine that would help prevent illness in children around the world. In her acceptance speech, Gwen gave credit to a former teacher for inspiring her to reach such a level of success. "I remember my fifth-grade teacher always told us to 'hitch your wagon to a star.' I never forgot that advice. When I became discouraged and thought my goal was unreachable, I just remembered that teacher's advice and kept on trying."

5. What is the best summary of this passage?
   Ⓐ Gwen received an award because she created a vaccine that helps prevent illness in children. In her acceptance speech, Gwen gave credit to a former teacher who had inspired her.
   Ⓑ By trying again and again, working long hours, and continuing despite setbacks, Gwen kept on trying.
   Ⓒ When Gwen became discouraged, she thought of the words of her fifth-grade teacher—"hitch your wagon to a star."
   Ⓓ Gwen worked long hours and often became discouraged because she thought her goal was unreachable. She reached her goal.

6. What is the best paraphrase of the first sentence in this passage?
   Ⓐ Gwen went to the auditorium to get a present.
   Ⓑ As many people watched, Gwen was presented with an award for her great achievements.
   Ⓒ A large audience filled the auditorium to see the show.
   Ⓓ Everyone wanted to go and watch Gwen stand in front of them and see what would happen.

GO ON

COMPREHENSION: Summarize and Paraphrase (continued)

Jerry had been saving money all summer to buy a new bicycle. His parents had said they would pay half the cost of the bike if he would earn the money to pay the other half. To earn his share, Jerry had been doing extra chores at home and had been helping the lady next door pull weeds each week.

One day in late August, there was an ad in the newspaper for the bike Jerry wanted. It was the lowest price he had ever seen for the bike, but he still didn't have enough money for his half. Jerry decided to talk to his dad about the problem, but he had trouble asking his dad to lend him the money.

"Stop beating around the bush, Jerry," Dad said. "I know you're trying to ask me to lend you the extra money for the bike so that you can buy it during the sale. I'll be happy to do that if you give me your word that you'll continue to earn the money to pay your half."

Jerry was overcome with joy, and he made a vow to repay his father in full.

7. Which of these ideas is most important to include in a summary of this story?
   - Ⓐ Jerry helped the lady next door pull weeds.
   - Ⓑ The ad was in the newspaper.
   - Ⓒ Jerry's parents had agreed to pay half the cost of the bike.
   - Ⓓ Jerry read about the bike he wanted late in the month of August.

8. What is the best paraphrase of the final sentence in this story?
   - Ⓐ Jerry was very happy, and he promised to pay back every cent to his father.
   - Ⓑ Jerry was joyful because of his father's kindness.
   - Ⓒ Jerry was glad his father didn't care about getting the money back.
   - Ⓓ Jerry's dad only gave him a few pennies, but Jerry was thankful.

STOP

Score _____

Harcourt • Reading and Language Skills Assessment

LITERARY RESPONSE AND ANALYSIS: Figurative Language

Directions: Read each passage. Fill in the answer circle in front of the correct answer for each question.

The turtle is a very interesting animal. Many turtles are only about the size of a cereal bowl. They are very good swimmers, but they are slow walkers. Watching a turtle walk is like watching ice melt. The turtle is also famous for its shell. A turtle's shell is its fortress. The turtle pulls its head and legs inside its shell when it senses danger.

9. Which group of words in this passage is a metaphor?
   Ⓐ very interesting animal
   Ⓑ good swimmers
   Ⓒ also famous
   Ⓓ shell is its fortress

10. The passage says watching a turtle walk is "like watching ice melt" because a turtle _____.
    Ⓐ is covered with water
    Ⓑ moves very slowly
    Ⓒ is very cold
    Ⓓ loves to sun itself

GO ON

LITERARY RESPONSE AND ANALYSIS: Figurative Language (continued)

> Mikel waited for his eyes to adjust to the deep darkness of the forest. He walked cautiously forward. The leaves were a thick blanket, covering the ground and muffling his steps. Finally, Mikel came to a small clearing and could see the clear blue sky overhead. The bright sunlight was like a comforting friend. He sat against the trunk of an old oak tree and took a drink of cool water from his canteen.

11. Which group of words in this story is a simile?

Ⓐ deep darkness

Ⓑ walked cautiously forward

Ⓒ came to a small clearing

Ⓓ sunlight was like a comforting friend

12. Which group of words in this story is a metaphor?

Ⓐ leaves were a thick blanket

Ⓑ clear blue sky overhead

Ⓒ an old oak tree

Ⓓ took a drink of cool water

STOP

Score _____

Distant Voyages / Theme 2

Harcourt • Reading and Language Skills Assessment

LANGUAGE

Directions: Read each pair of simple sentences. Choose the answer that shows the best way to combine the simple sentences.

13. That author has written many novels. Three of them have sold more than a million copies.

    Ⓐ That author has written many novels, three of them have sold more than a million copies.

    Ⓑ That author has written many novels but three of them have sold more than a million copies.

    Ⓒ That author has written many novels, or three of them have sold more than a million copies.

    Ⓓ That author has written many novels, and three of them have sold more than a million copies.

14. The California condor was close to extinction. It has begun to recover.

    Ⓐ The California condor was close to extinction but; it has begun to recover.

    Ⓑ The California condor was close to extinction, but it has begun to recover.

    Ⓒ The California condor was close to extinction, or it has begun to recover.

    Ⓓ The California condor was close to extinction and, it has begun to recover.

Harcourt • Reading and Language Skills Assessment

GO ON

LANGUAGE (continued)

Directions: Choose the answer that best describes the underlined words in each sentence.

15. After the Mars Pathfinder landed on the planet Mars, it sent many pictures back to scientists on Earth.
    Ⓐ independent clause
    Ⓑ compound sentence
    Ⓒ dependent clause
    Ⓓ coordinating conjunction

16. Because Jupiter's gravity is greater than Earth's, a person would feel heavier on Jupiter.
    Ⓐ simple sentence
    Ⓑ complex sentence
    Ⓒ compound sentence
    Ⓓ dependent clause

Directions: Read each pair of sentences. Choose the answer that shows the best way to combine the sentences to form a complex sentence.

17. A volcano explodes. The event is called an eruption.
    Ⓐ When a volcano explodes, the event is called an eruption.
    Ⓑ Before a volcano explodes, the event is called an eruption.
    Ⓒ A volcano explodes, or the event is called an eruption.
    Ⓓ The volcano explodes; the volcano erupts.

18. The Science Center is popular. It has a new exhibit about dinosaurs.
    Ⓐ Until the Science Center is popular; it has a new dinosaur exhibit.
    Ⓑ The Science Center has a new exhibit about dinosaurs, it is popular.
    Ⓒ The Science Center is popular because it has a new exhibit about dinosaurs.
    Ⓓ Although the Science Center has a new exhibit about dinosaurs, it is popular.

GO ON

Harcourt • Reading and Language Skills Assessment

LANGUAGE (continued)

Directions: Read each sentence. Choose the proper noun or abbreviation that should be capitalized in each.

19. Each <u>fourth</u> of July our <u>family</u> watches <u>fireworks</u> in the city <u>park</u>.

   Ⓐ fourth

   Ⓑ family

   Ⓒ fireworks

   Ⓓ park

20. When I had the <u>flu</u>, <u>dr.</u> Gonzales gave me a <u>prescription</u> for some <u>medicine</u>.

   Ⓐ flu

   Ⓑ dr.

   Ⓒ prescription

   Ⓓ medicine

Directions: Choose the plural noun that is written correctly.

21. Ⓐ boxs

   Ⓑ churchs

   Ⓒ waltzes

   Ⓓ wishs

22. Ⓐ tomatos

   Ⓑ lifes

   Ⓒ vallies

   Ⓓ mysteries

STOP

Team Work / Theme 2
Reading and Language Skills Assessment

Harcourt

Orlando   Boston   Dallas   Chicago   San Diego

Part No. 9997-37763-X

ISBN 0-15-332204-7 (Package of 12)

5

TROPHIES

Reading and Language Skills Assessment Posttest

Distant Voyages/Theme 2

Name _____ Date _____

SKILL AREA	Criterion Score	Pupil Score	Pupil Strength
COMPREHENSION			
Draw Conclusions	3/4	_____	_____
Summarize and Paraphrase	3/4	_____	_____
LITERARY RESPONSE AND ANALYSIS			
Figurative Language	3/4	_____	_____
LANGUAGE	7/10	_____	_____
Simple and Compound Sentences			
Clauses			
Complex Sentences			
Common and Proper Nouns; Abbreviations			
Singular and Plural Nouns		_____	_____
TOTAL SCORE	16/22		

Were accommodations made in administering this test? ☐ Yes ☐ No

Type of accommodations: _____

_____

Printed in the United States of America

ISBN 0-15-332204-7

9 10   170   10 09 08 07 06 05

COMPREHENSION: Draw Conclusions

Directions: Read each passage. Fill in the answer circle in front of the correct answer for each question.

Aerobic exercises are activities that cause you to breathe deeply and make your heart beat quickly for at least twenty minutes. The exercises are done at medium speed and make your heart, other muscles, and lungs physically fit. Examples include jumping rope, riding a bicycle, fast walking, and swimming. Aerobic exercises also help relieve stress, which is a tense feeling you get when things bother you or when you get in an argument.

To make your aerobic exercise safer and more healthful, you should warm up beforehand and cool down afterward. Warm-up activities, such as stretching, get your muscles ready to work. Cool-down activities, which include stretching, slowly pedaling your bicycle, or walking, let your muscles slowly relax as your pulse and breathing return to normal.

1. According to the passage, if you were angry at a friend, you would feel better if you _____.
   - Ⓐ yelled at your friend
   - Ⓑ counted to ten
   - Ⓒ took a long bike ride
   - Ⓓ worried about something else

2. The best way to perform an aerobic activity is to _____.
   - Ⓐ exercise for about five minutes
   - Ⓑ begin and end the exercise slowly
   - Ⓒ do the activity as quickly as possible
   - Ⓓ exercise until your muscles hurt

GO ON

COMPREHENSION: Draw Conclusions (continued)

Every December for more than 100 years, people have gone outside to count birds. They count birds in the United States, Canada, parts of Central and South America, and on several islands. This is called the Christmas Bird Count, although it is not always done on Christmas. Why do people do this? Because it gives scientists information about how different bird species are doing. It also tells scientists something about the environment. The bird counters have to list each kind of bird they see by name. In some places, like Mad Island Marsh in Texas, this means listing more than 200 kinds of birds.

The bird counters start before sunrise. Usually they work in teams to help each other identify the birds they see. The bird counters take binoculars and bird books. They also take warm clothing and food, because they are outdoors all day. They have to be quiet as they walk through the woods or marshes. The bird counters get tired by the end of the day, but they like what they do. One of them said that the Christmas Bird Count was like a "nature treasure hunt."

3. Based on this passage, you can conclude that almost all the bird counters _____.
   Ⓐ enjoy their outing
   Ⓑ see very few birds
   Ⓒ are close friends
   Ⓓ make a lot of money

4. Based on this passage, you can conclude that the bird counters report their findings to _____.
   Ⓐ relatives
   Ⓑ newspapers
   Ⓒ hunters
   Ⓓ scientists

Harcourt • Reading and Language Skills Assessment

STOP

COMPREHENSION: Summarize and Paraphrase

Directions: Read each passage. Fill in the answer circle in front of the correct answer for each question.

The Johnson family has a new member. The new family member is not a baby or a pet. Instead, the newcomer is a teenager from Switzerland. His name is Antonio Moretti. He is an exchange student from an Italian-speaking region of Switzerland. He will be living with the Johnson family for one year and going to school here in the United States. He hopes to improve his English, and he would like to learn how to play American football.

"I am very happy to be here in the United States," said Antonio, or Tony, as he likes to be called.

The Johnson family is happy to host Antonio. They will help him improve his English. They will also instruct Antonio in the beliefs and customs of the United States.

5. What is the best summary of this passage?
   Ⓐ The teenager, Antonio Moretti says, "I am very happy to be here in the United States."
   Ⓑ The Johnson family has a new member. He is not a baby. His name is Antonio Moretti, but he likes to be called Tony.
   Ⓒ Antonio Moretti, or Tony, an exchange student from an Italian-speaking region of Switzerland, will live with the Johnson family for a year. He hopes to improve his English and to learn how to play American football.
   Ⓓ Antonio Moretti is an exchange student. He speaks Italian. He will live with the Johnson family here in the United States. He will go to school here in the United States.

6. What is the best paraphrase of the final sentence in this passage?
   Ⓐ The family will teach Antonio how to live.
   Ⓑ They will also show Antonio a map of the United States.
   Ⓒ The family wants to make sure that Antonio has a fun time.
   Ⓓ They will also help Antonio learn how Americans think and act.

COMPREHENSION: Summarize and Paraphrase (continued)

People have been trying to take care of their teeth for thousands of years. Gold toothpicks that are more than 5,000 years old have been found in ancient places in the Middle East. In the 1700s, toothbrushes were made from twigs, plant roots, or animal hairs. Most products for cleaning teeth were powders that usually were made by mixing plants with oils and adding powdered charcoal, chalk, or baking soda.

Modern dentists have learned that germs and bacteria are the worst enemies of our teeth and gums. Toothpastes and gels contain materials that stop the growth of these tiny enemies. Toothpaste companies add flavors, such as peppermint, to improve taste.

The most important thing you can do for your teeth is to brush and floss at least twice a day. It's also a good idea to limit your intake of candy and other sugar-rich foods.

7. Which of these ideas is most important to include in a summary of this passage?

Ⓐ People have taken care of their teeth for thousands of years.

Ⓑ Some ancient toothpicks have been found.

Ⓒ Germs and bacteria are tiny.

Ⓓ Peppermint is one flavor added to toothpaste.

8. What is the best paraphrase of the final sentence in this passage?

Ⓐ You would be wise to eat lots of candy.

Ⓑ It's also a good idea to eat less candy and other sweets.

Ⓒ It's a great idea to limit the amount of food you eat.

Ⓓ A smart person would never again eat sugar.

STOP

LITERARY RESPONSE AND ANALYSIS: Figurative Language

Directions: Read each passage. Fill in the answer circle in front of the correct answer for each question.

Chris and his father pointed their telescope up into the night sky. The stars were diamonds in the darkness. Chris could see the Big Dipper, The North Star, and the planet Venus. But Chris's favorite thing to look at was the moon. To Chris, the moon looked like a saucer of milk. He stood quite still and gazed at the white, glowing orb.

9. Which group of words in this story is a simile?
Ⓐ into the night sky
Ⓑ was the moon
Ⓒ moon looked like a saucer of milk
Ⓓ stood quite still and gazed

10. The story says that the stars "were diamonds in the darkness" because diamonds _____.
Ⓐ are valuable
Ⓑ have sharp points
Ⓒ are small but strong
Ⓓ twinkle and shine

GO ON

Harcourt • Reading and Language Skills Assessment

LITERARY RESPONSE AND ANALYSIS: Figurative Language (continued)

> This was Sally's first spelling bee. Although she had studied hard, she was very nervous. She could barely stand up, and her stomach was a churning sea of fear. When Sally's teacher asked her to spell her first word, her body was like a leaf in the wind. However, her studying paid off because she spelled the word perfectly. Sally's teacher smiled and said, "Nicely done!" After this, Sally relaxed and enjoyed the contest.

11. Which group of words in this story is a metaphor?

Ⓐ was very nervous

Ⓑ stomach was a churning sea

Ⓒ spelled the word perfectly

Ⓓ relaxed and enjoyed the contest

12. The story says that Sally's body was "like a leaf in the wind" because she was most probably _____.

Ⓐ shaking

Ⓑ small

Ⓒ thin and light

Ⓓ wearing green

STOP

Score _____

Harcourt • Reading and Language Skills Assessment

LANGUAGE

Directions: Read each pair of simple sentences. Choose the answer that shows the best way to combine the simple sentences.

13. We can ride the bus across town. We can go in the family car.

Ⓐ We can ride the bus across town but we can go in the family car.

Ⓑ We can ride the bus across town, or we can go in the family car.

Ⓒ We can ride the bus across town, we can go in the family car.

Ⓓ We can ride the bus across town but; we can go in the family car.

14. Tanya is an excellent skater. She has won several skating contests.

Ⓐ Tanya is an excellent skater; or she has won several skating contests.

Ⓑ Tanya is an excellent skater she, has won several skating contests.

Ⓒ Tanya is an excellent skater, but she has won several skating contests.

Ⓓ Tanya is an excellent skater, and she has won several skating contests.

GO ON

LANGUAGE (continued)

Directions: Choose the answer that best describes the underlined words in each sentence.

15. Manatees are called <u>gentle giants</u> because they are large, harmless animals.
    Ⓐ independent clause
    Ⓑ compound sentence
    Ⓒ dependent clause
    Ⓓ coordinating conjunction

16. <u>If we recycle metal, glass, and paper</u>, we can help to conserve our natural resources.
    Ⓐ independent clause
    Ⓑ coordinating conjunction
    Ⓒ subordinating conjunction
    Ⓓ dependent clause

Directions: Read each pair of sentences. Choose the answer that shows the best way to combine the sentences to form a complex sentence.

17. The caterpillar is inside the cocoon. It changes into a butterfly.
    Ⓐ The caterpillar is inside the cocoon, it changes into a butterfly.
    Ⓑ While the caterpillar is inside the cocoon, it changes into a butterfly.
    Ⓒ The caterpillar and butterfly are inside the cocoon and change.
    Ⓓ The caterpillar is inside the cocoon; although it changes into a butterfly.

18. The hikers checked their supply of food and water. They started off.
    Ⓐ Before they started off, the hikers checked their supply of food and water.
    Ⓑ They started off, or they checked their supply of food and water.
    Ⓒ Since they started off; they checked their supply of food and water.
    Ⓓ Because the hikers had a supply and they started to check food and water.

GO ON

LANGUAGE (continued)

Directions: Read each sentence. Choose the proper noun or abbreviation that should be capitalized in each.

19. The birthday <u>party</u> for my <u>friend</u> Myra is being held at her neighborhood <u>pool</u> on Maplewood <u>ave</u>.

Ⓐ party

Ⓑ friend

Ⓒ pool

Ⓓ ave.

20. The first <u>cowboys</u> in this <u>country</u> were Mexican <u>americans</u> with great skills in <u>horsemanship</u>.

Ⓐ cowboys

Ⓑ country

Ⓒ americans

Ⓓ horsemanship

Directions: Choose the plural noun that is written correctly.

21. Ⓐ mice

Ⓑ tooths

Ⓒ childs

Ⓓ foots

22. Ⓐ armys

Ⓑ soldieres

Ⓒ troopes

Ⓓ men

STOP

Team Work / Theme 2
Reading and Language Skills Assessment

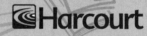

Orlando   Boston   Dallas   Chicago   San Diego

Part No. 9997-37757-5

ISBN 0-15-332204-7 (Package of 12)

TROPHIES

Reading and Language Skills
Assessment Pretest

Distant Voyages / Theme 3

Name _____ Date _____

SKILL AREA	Criterion Score	Pupil Score	Pupil Strength
COMPREHENSION			
Text Structure: Main Idea and Details	3/4	_____	_____
Text Structure: Sequence	3/4	_____	_____
RESEARCH AND INFORMATION SKILLS			
Graphic Aids	3/4	_____	_____
LANGUAGE	7/10	_____	_____
Possessive Nouns			
Pronouns and Antecedents			
Subject and Object Pronouns			
Possessive Pronouns			
Case			
TOTAL SCORE	16/22	_____	_____

Were accommodations made in administering this test? ❑ Yes ❑ No

Type of accommodations: _____

_____

Harcourt • Reading and Language Skills Assessment

COMPREHENSION: Text Structure: Main Idea and Details

Directions: Read the passage. Fill in the answer circle in front of the correct answer for each question.

Potatoes are vegetables. They are grown in many places and eaten in many forms. They are also used to make other products, such as certain types of flour. In North America, the state of Maine and the Canadian province of Prince Edward Island are known for their potato farms.

The part of the potato that people eat is called a "tuber." It grows in the ground but is not part of the root. Most potatoes are round or shaped like an oval. However, some potatoes with very unusual shapes have been discovered.

In the United States today, a tremendous amount of potatoes are eaten in the form of potato chips and "French fries." However, some food experts warn that frying food makes it less healthy than other methods of preparation. Potatoes can be a very good source of vitamins and minerals. So, the next time you eat a baked, boiled, or roasted potato, you can feel confident that you are having a healthy food.

1. What is the main idea of this passage?
   - Ⓐ Most potatoes are round or oval-shaped.
   - Ⓑ The potato is an important vegetable.
   - Ⓒ Potatoes are used to make flour.
   - Ⓓ The state of Maine is known for its potato farms.

2. Which detail, if added to the passage, would best support the main idea?
   - Ⓐ Potatoes can be dried or frozen.
   - Ⓑ French fries are often served with hamburgers.
   - Ⓒ A potato is about 80 percent water and 20 percent solid.
   - Ⓓ The potato is a major food source for people worldwide.

GO ON

COMPREHENSION: Text Structure: Main Idea and Details (continued)

3. According to the passage, a baked potato is a healthy source of _____.

Ⓐ vitamins

Ⓑ sugar

Ⓒ fat

Ⓓ flour

4. Which detail could best be added to paragraph 3?

Ⓐ The starch in potatoes gives our bodies energy.

Ⓑ Prince Edward Island is in eastern Canada.

Ⓒ Most people eat the roots of carrot plants.

Ⓓ Some farmers grow potatoes that are very large.

STOP

Harcourt • Reading and Language Skills Assessment

COMPREHENSION: Text Structure: Sequence

Directions: Read the passage. Fill in the answer circle in front of the correct answer for each question.

Ivan arrived at the gym before anyone else. He waited outside until Coach O'Neil came and unlocked the doors. Ivan helped the coach sweep the floor. When they were done sweeping, they set up the volleyball nets. By the time they finished, the other players on the team had arrived. They had a team meeting in which they discussed what they would need to do in the game against the Winston Rams.

Just as the meeting ended, the Rams arrived. After both teams warmed up, the game began. The Rams won the first game 21 to 12. Coach O'Neil held a quick huddle with her team. She reminded them to stick to the game plan. Ivan's team won the rest of the games and the match. All the players shook hands. Then the Rams got back in their van and drove off.

The players on Ivan's team stayed behind to help take down the nets and store them away. Then Coach O'Neil invited everyone out for ice cream. She let the players use the phone in her office to call their parents for permission. After everyone checked in at home, the coach treated the entire squad to sundaes.

5. Who arrived at the gym first?
Ⓐ Coach O'Neil
Ⓑ Ivan
Ⓒ Ivan's teammates
Ⓓ the Rams

6. What did Ivan do **right after** he entered the gym?
Ⓐ He warmed up with the other players.
Ⓑ He attended a meeting with his teammates.
Ⓒ He helped set up the volleyball nets.
Ⓓ He helped the coach sweep the floor.

GO ON

COMPREHENSION: Text Structure: Sequence (continued)

7. What did Coach O'Neil do **right after** the first game?
   Ⓐ She held a quick huddle.
   Ⓑ She cleaned the floor.
   Ⓒ She made phone calls.
   Ⓓ She talked to the Rams.

8. What happened **last** in the story?
   Ⓐ Ivan's team won the match.
   Ⓑ Coach O'Neil took the team for ice cream.
   Ⓒ The players used Coach O'Neil's phone.
   Ⓓ The players helped Coach O'Neil put things away.

STOP

RESEARCH AND INFORMATION SKILLS: Graphic Aids

Directions: Study the pie chart. Then fill in the answer circle in front of the correct answer for each question.

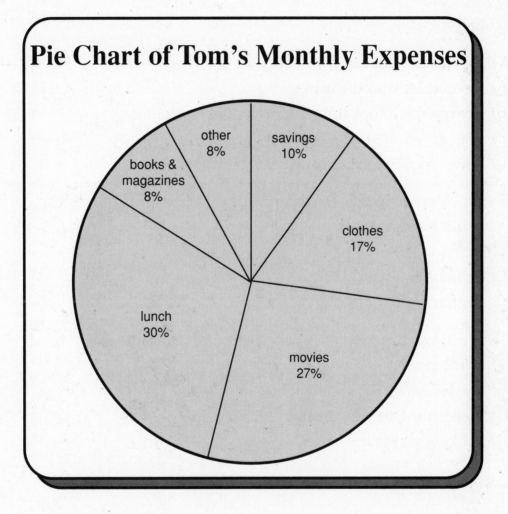

Pie Chart of Tom's Monthly Expenses

- other 8%
- savings 10%
- books & magazines 8%
- clothes 17%
- lunch 30%
- movies 27%

GO ON

RESEARCH AND INFORMATION SKILLS: Graphic Aids (continued)

9. On which monthly expense does Tom spend the most?
   (A) savings
   (B) clothes
   (C) movies
   (D) lunch

10. What percent of his monthly expenses does Tom spend on clothes?
   (A) 8%
   (B) 17%
   (C) 27%
   (D) 30%

11. On which expense does Tom spend 10% of his monthly budget?
   (A) books & magazines
   (B) other
   (C) savings
   (D) clothes

12. On which two expenses does Tom spend the same amount?
   (A) other, savings
   (B) movies, lunch
   (C) books & magazines, clothes
   (D) books & magazines, other

STOP

Harcourt • Reading and Language Skills Assessment

LANGUAGE

Directions: Choose the correct possessive noun or plural noun to complete each sentence.

13. We watched as the _____ last rays sank beneath the horizon.
    - (A) suns'
    - (B) suns
    - (C) sun's
    - (D) suns's

14. The new _____ TV show is also popular with adults.
    - (A) childrens's
    - (B) childrens'
    - (C) childrens
    - (D) children's

15. The _____ of the maple trees were yellow, orange, and red.
    - (A) leaves
    - (B) leaves'
    - (C) leafs'
    - (D) leaf's

16. My oldest _____ room is vacant since he went away to college.
    - (A) brothers
    - (B) brother's
    - (C) brothers'
    - (D) brothers's

GO ON ▶

LANGUAGE (continued)

Directions: Choose the answer that best describes the underlined word in each sentence.

17. Our teacher told <u>us</u> that the Statue of Liberty was a gift from the people of France.
Ⓐ subject pronoun; singular
Ⓑ subject pronoun; plural
Ⓒ object pronoun; singular
Ⓓ object pronoun; plural

18. <u>They</u> gazed in awe at the gigantic dinosaur skeleton on display in the museum.
Ⓐ subject pronoun; singular
Ⓑ subject pronoun; plural
Ⓒ object pronoun; singular
Ⓓ object pronoun; plural

Directions: Choose the answer that gives the **antecedent** of the underlined pronoun in each sentence.

19. The doctors studied their notes before <u>they</u> entered the patient's room.
Ⓐ doctors
Ⓑ studied
Ⓒ notes
Ⓓ room

20. The researchers have created a new medicine, and most people can afford to buy <u>it</u>.
Ⓐ researchers
Ⓑ medicine
Ⓒ people
Ⓓ afford

GO ON ▶

LANGUAGE (continued)

Directions: Choose the possessive pronoun that correctly completes each sentence.

21. After winning the city championship, the basketball players celebrated with _____ coach.
    Ⓐ his
    Ⓑ ours
    Ⓒ their
    Ⓓ my

22. Jacob has a good batting average, but _____ is better.
    Ⓐ mine
    Ⓑ its
    Ⓒ your
    Ⓓ my

STOP

· TROPHIES ·

A Changing Planet / Theme 3
Reading and Language Skills Assessment

Harcourt

Orlando   Boston   Dallas   Chicago   San Diego

Part No. 9997-37764-8

ISBN 0-15-332204-7 (Package of 12)

TROPHIES

Reading and Language Skills Assessment Posttest

Distant Voyages / Theme 3

Name _____ Date _____

SKILL AREA	Criterion Score	Pupil Score	Pupil Strength
COMPREHENSION			
Text Structure: Main Idea and Details	3/4	_____	_____
Text Structure: Sequence	3/4	_____	_____
RESEARCH AND INFORMATION SKILLS			
Graphic Aids	3/4	_____	_____
LANGUAGE Possessive Nouns Pronouns and Antecedents Subject and Object Pronouns Possessive Pronouns Case	7/10	_____	_____
TOTAL SCORE	16/22	_____	_____

Were accommodations made in administering this test? ☐ Yes ☐ No

Type of accommodations: _____

_____

Harcourt • Reading and Language Skills Assessment

COMPREHENSION: Text Structure: Main Idea and Details

Directions: Read the passage. Fill in the answer circle in front of the correct answer for each question.

The word *glove* comes from an old Anglo Saxon word that means "the palm of the hand." The earliest gloves may have been worn by cave people. In ancient Greece people wore gloves to protect their hands when they did hard work.

During some periods in history, gloves became a symbol of wealth or authority. During the Middle Ages, gloves were mostly worn by rich people. If a knight threw down his glove in front of another knight, it was understood to be a challenge to fight. If the other knight picked it up, he accepted the challenge.

Today gloves are worn by many people for many different purposes. Gloves keep hands warm in cold weather. They protect workers from hot, cold, or dangerous materials. Sometimes they are still worn as a kind of fashion statement.

1. What is the main idea of this passage?
   (A) People have worn gloves throughout history.
   (B) In Greece, people wore gloves when they did hard work.
   (C) Gloves may be worn for fashion.
   (D) In the Middle Ages, rich people wore gloves.

2. Which detail, if added to the passage, would best support the main idea?
   (A) Wool gloves are usually warmer than cotton gloves.
   (B) The Romans used gloves for fashion and to show rank.
   (C) New York City was a major center for glove making.
   (D) Women's gloves are often very expensive.

GO ON

COMPREHENSION: Text Structure: Main Idea and Details (continued)

3. A knight who picked up a glove thrown down by another knight would soon _____.

   Ⓐ build a castle

   Ⓑ leave on a journey

   Ⓒ attend a feast

   Ⓓ be in a fight

4. Which detail could best be added to paragraph 3?

   Ⓐ A knight would sometimes wear a lady's glove on his helmet.

   Ⓑ Some gloves can protect a worker's hands from acid.

   Ⓒ Early cave dwellers lived in present-day France.

   Ⓓ The world's first great poets lived in ancient Greece.

STOP

Score _____

COMPREHENSION: Text Structure: Sequence

Directions: Read the passage. Fill in the answer circle in front of the correct answer for each question.

It was Saturday, and Tasha had a busy day. She woke up at 7:00 A.M., dressed, and then ate breakfast. After that, Tasha watched TV until her aunt arrived to cut her hair. This took longer than expected, and Tasha and her mother had to hurry to make Tasha's 10:30 A.M. dental appointment. After the dentist, they dropped by the library to return a book, and then they stopped for lunch. Next they went straight to Tasha's piano lesson, and afterward to the store to buy Tasha a new dress for her birthday party.

After dinner that evening, Tasha asked if she could help her mother alter her birthday dress, but her mother replied, "I can't tonight, Tasha. Besides, you need to help me put away the dishes. Then you need to work on your book report; finally, you need to take a bath before going to bed. We'll alter your dress one evening next week."

5. What did Tasha do **right after** she got dressed?
- (A) went shopping
- (B) had her hair cut
- (C) watched TV
- (D) ate breakfast

6. What did Tasha do **right after** leaving the dentist's office?
- (A) bought a dress
- (B) ate lunch
- (C) returned a library book
- (D) had a piano lesson

GO ON

COMPREHENSION: Text Structure: Sequence (continued)

7. What did Tasha's mother want her to do **last** in the story?
   - Ⓐ eat dinner
   - Ⓑ take a bath
   - Ⓒ work on a report
   - Ⓓ put away the dishes

8. Which of these things will have to wait until next week?
   - Ⓐ altering the dress
   - Ⓑ going shopping
   - Ⓒ playing the piano
   - Ⓓ washing the dishes

STOP

Score _____

Harcourt • Reading and Language Skills Assessment

RESEARCH AND INFORMATION SKILLS: Graphic Aids

Directions: Study the chart and map. Then fill in the answer circle in front of the correct answer for each question.

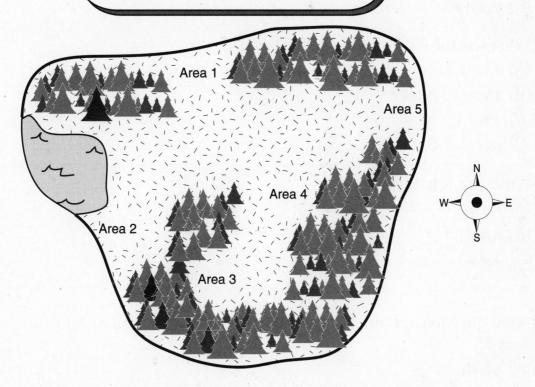

Map of Pine City Park

Mrs. Lima's class visited Pine City Park. They recorded the number of different kinds of birds they saw in different areas of the park.

Birds Seen by Mrs. Lima's Class at Pine City Park

	Area 1	Area 2	Area 3	Area 4	Area 5	Total
Robins	4	4	2	1	5	16
Cardinals	3	1	2	2	2	10
Sparrows	1	0	0	0	2	3
Crows	4	3	5	5	5	22
Blue Jays	1	1	4	3	6	15
Total	13	9	13	11	20	

GO ON

RESEARCH AND INFORMATION SKILLS: Graphic Aids (continued)

9. Which bird was seen the most times during the visit?

Ⓐ Crow

Ⓑ Cardinal

Ⓒ Sparrow

Ⓓ Robin

10. What was the total number of birds seen?

Ⓐ 13

Ⓑ 16

Ⓒ 22

Ⓓ 66

11. What area is farthest east?

Ⓐ Area 1

Ⓑ Area 2

Ⓒ Area 3

Ⓓ Area 5

12. What direction did the class **mostly** have to walk to go from Area 1 to Area 2?

Ⓐ north

Ⓑ east

Ⓒ southwest

Ⓓ northwest

STOP

Harcourt • Reading and Language Skills Assessment

LANGUAGE

Directions: Choose the correct possessive noun or plural noun to complete each sentence.

13. A _____ ears are large, triangular, and furry.
    Ⓐ fox
    Ⓑ fox's
    Ⓒ foxes
    Ⓓ foxes's

14. Many _____ go to theme parts during their summer vacations.
    Ⓐ family's
    Ⓑ families'
    Ⓒ families
    Ⓓ familys's

15. Several _____ fruit trees were damaged by the freezing temperatures.
    Ⓐ farmers'
    Ⓑ farmers's
    Ⓒ farmer
    Ⓓ farmers

16. A _____ webbed feet and flippers make it a marvelous swimmer.
    Ⓐ penguin
    Ⓑ penguin's
    Ⓒ penguins
    Ⓓ penguins'

GO ON

LANGUAGE (continued)

Directions: Choose the answer that best describes the underlined word in each sentence.

17. My father wants <u>me</u> to follow in his footsteps and become a lawyer.
    (A) subject pronoun; singular
    (B) subject pronoun; plural
    (C) object pronoun; singular
    (D) object pronoun; plural

18. Derek, Anna, and <u>I</u> are members of our school's chess club.
    (A) subject pronoun; singular
    (B) subject pronoun; plural
    (C) object pronoun; singular
    (D) object pronoun; plural

Directions: Choose the answer that gives the **antecedent** of the underlined pronoun in each sentence.

19. After the Revolutionary War, colonists were afraid that a strong national government might impose strict laws on <u>them</u>.
    (A) Revolutionary War
    (B) colonists
    (C) government
    (D) laws

20. Texas was known as the Lone Star Republic because, in 1839, <u>it</u> adopted a flag with a single white star.
    (A) Texas
    (B) flag
    (C) single
    (D) star

GO ON

Distant Voyages / Theme 3

LANGUAGE (continued)

Directions: Choose the possessive pronoun that correctly completes each sentence.

21. Carla's friends have come up with a good idea for a fund-raiser, but we think _____ idea will make more money.
    - Ⓐ mine
    - Ⓑ theirs
    - Ⓒ our
    - Ⓓ its

22. A group's success depends on the ability of _____ members to work together.
    - Ⓐ theirs
    - Ⓑ yours
    - Ⓒ his
    - Ⓓ its

STOP

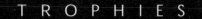

A Changing Planet / Theme 3
Reading and Language Skills Assessment

Harcourt

Orlando   Boston   Dallas   Chicago   San Diego

Part No. 9997-37758-3

ISBN 0-15-332204-7 (Package of 12)

5

TROPHIES

Mid-Year Reading and Language Skills Assessment

Distant Voyages/Themes 1, 2, 3

Name _____ Date _____

SKILL AREA	Criterion Score	Pupil Score	Comments
VOCABULARY (Items 1–4)	3/4	___/4	_____
COMPREHENSION (Items 5–14)	7/10	___/10	_____
LITERARY RESPONSE AND ANALYSIS (Items 15–20)	4/6	___/6	_____
RESEARCH AND INFORMATION SKILLS (Items 21–24)	3/4	___/4	_____
LANGUAGE (Items 25–36)	9/12	___/12	_____
TOTAL SCORE	**26/36**	___/36	_____

Were accommodations made in administering this test? ☐ Yes ☐ No

Type of accommodations: _____

_____

Harcourt • Reading and Language Skills Assessment

VOCABULARY

Directions: Read each sentence. Fill in the answer circle in front of the correct answer for each question.

1. Which prefix should be added to the word *activate* to make it mean "the opposite of activate"?
   Ⓐ *co-*
   Ⓑ *de-*
   Ⓒ *mis-*
   Ⓓ *pre-*

2. Which suffix should be added to the word *courtesy* to make it mean "full of courtesy"?
   Ⓐ *-or*
   Ⓑ *-ing*
   Ⓒ *-ous*
   Ⓓ *-er*

3. Which suffix should be added to the word *abandon* to make it mean "the act of abandoning"?
   Ⓐ *-ment*
   Ⓑ *-er*
   Ⓒ *-ous*
   Ⓓ *-ful*

4. Which root word means *hand*?
   Ⓐ "man" as in **manicure**
   Ⓑ "micro" as in **microgram**
   Ⓒ "graph" as in **phonograph**
   Ⓓ "bio" as in **biology**

STOP

Harcourt • Reading and Language Skills Assessment

COMPREHENSION

Directions: Read each passage. Fill in the answer circle in front of the correct answer for each question.

One good decision you can make to stay healthy is to get plenty of exercise. *Exercise* is any activity that makes your body work hard. Exercise helps make your heart and muscles strong. To exercise, you can choose an activity that you enjoy doing alone, such as swimming, or you can choose an activity you enjoy doing with others, such as playing tennis.

Some people forget that *rest* is important to good health, too. Getting enough rest is another good decision you need to make to stay healthy. After you exercise or play for a while, you usually begin to feel tired. Feeling tired is your body's signal to slow down and get some rest. When you rest, you move your body as little as possible and think about something pleasant. Resting allows your body to use less energy. Your heart, muscles, and lungs get a chance to relax. There are many different ways that you can rest. Reading a good story, playing a board game you enjoy, or sitting quietly and daydreaming are all good ways to rest.

Another good health decision you can make is to get enough sleep. How much sleep you need varies from person to person, but you need to sleep part of every day. When you sleep, your whole body rests—even your brain. Your body still uses energy, but it uses less than it does when you are awake and active. While you sleep, your body works to store energy for you to use the next day.

GO ON

Distant Voyages / Mid-Year Skills

COMPREHENSION (continued)

5. What is the main idea of this passage?
   - Ⓐ After you exercise or play for a while, your body feels tired.
   - Ⓑ You can choose an activity you enjoy doing alone.
   - Ⓒ When you rest, you move your body as little as possible.
   - Ⓓ Staying healthy involves making a lot of good decisions.

6. The passage says that exercise is important because it _____.
   - Ⓐ helps your lungs relax
   - Ⓑ slows down your heart
   - Ⓒ lets your brain rest
   - Ⓓ makes your muscles strong

7. According to the passage, a good way to rest your body would be to _____.
   - Ⓐ practice jumping rope
   - Ⓑ sit down and listen to music
   - Ⓒ ride a bike with friends
   - Ⓓ run in a relay race

8. From the information in this passage, you could conclude that _____.
   - Ⓐ if you get plenty of sleep, you do not need to exercise
   - Ⓑ exercise, rest, and sleep are all important to good health
   - Ⓒ it is better to exercise alone than with others
   - Ⓓ everyone needs the same amount of sleep each day

GO ON

COMPREHENSION (continued)

Max cheered up instantly when he saw who was at the door. The Cole brothers, who lived in the next town, were standing in the doorway with Spike. The last time Max had seen Spike was a week ago when Spike ran off chasing squirrels. After Spike had been gone several hours, Max began to worry. After a few days Max had almost given up hope of ever seeing his dog again. Now Max was filled with joy as the Cole brothers led Spike on a leash and returned him to Max. As soon as Spike saw Max, he began to lick his owner in happy greeting. While Spike expressed his happiness, Max counted out ten one-dollar bills, which was the reward he had offered to anyone who could find and return his missing pet.

Later, Max administered a serious verbal reprimand to Spike for vanishing. Max tried his best to be serious, but Spike just barked happily and licked Max's face. Max laughed and said, "I'm happy to see you, too, Spike. How about a dog treat to celebrate your return?" Spike barked a "yes," and they headed for the kitchen together.

9. What is the best summary of this passage?
   Ⓐ The last time Max had seen Spike had been a week ago when Spike ran off chasing squirrels. Max began to worry after Spike had been gone several hours.
   Ⓑ Spike had been missing for a week since the day he disappeared while chasing squirrels. Max was delighted to see him again, and Spike licked his owner in a happy greeting.
   Ⓒ Max cheered up quickly when he saw that the Cole brothers, who lived in the next town, were standing at his door. He gave them a ten-dollar reward. Spike got a treat.
   Ⓓ Max was overjoyed when his dog Spike, who had been missing for a week, was returned by the Cole brothers from the next town. As Spike licked him, Max counted out a ten-dollar reward. Later, Max gave Spike a dog treat to celebrate.

10. What is the best paraphrase of the first sentence of paragraph 2?
    Ⓐ Later, Max talked to Spike.
    Ⓑ Later, Max told Spike that Max was angry with him.
    Ⓒ Later, Max scolded Spike for disappearing.
    Ⓓ Later, Max gave Spike a lecture.

GO ON

Distant Voyages / Mid-Year Skills

COMPREHENSION (continued)

Robert E. Peary, an American explorer, is famous for discovering the North Pole. Peary was interested in exploring the uncharted Arctic regions. In 1891 the Philadelphia Academy of Natural Sciences put him in charge of an expedition to Greenland. His explorations on this trip allowed him to prove that Greenland is an island. Peary made important scientific discoveries during other expeditions he undertook in the 1890s. In 1898 he published a book, *Northward over the Great Ice*, in which he described his journeys.

In 1897 Peary set forth on a four-year journey that he hoped would result in the discovery of the North Pole. He did not succeed in finding the Pole during that mission, but he did travel farther north in the American Arctic than anyone had ever been before.

In July of 1908, Peary set out again for the North Pole on a specially built ship called the *Roosevelt*. The hardships of the expedition were so great and supplies so short that many members of his team had to turn back. When Peary finally reached the Pole in early April of 1909, he had with him only four Eskimos and his loyal assistant Matthew Henson, an African American explorer. They spent only thirty hours at the Pole before beginning the journey back to the *Roosevelt*.

Excitement about Peary reaching the North Pole was cut short because another explorer, Frederick Cook, announced a week before Peary's return that *he* had reached the Pole a year before Peary. The United States Congress investigated Cook's claim, but they wound up giving Peary credit for the discovery. Peary wrote about his historic expedition in a book called *The North Pole*, published in 1910.

11. When did Peary reach the North Pole?
- Ⓐ before he proved Greenland is an island
- Ⓑ during a four-year journey that began in 1897
- Ⓒ after he set sail on the *Roosevelt* in 1908
- Ⓓ before he published *Northward over the Great Ice* in 1898

12. Which of these happened **after** Peary reached the North Pole?
- Ⓐ Congress investigated Cook's claim about reaching the Pole first.
- Ⓑ Peary set out in July on a specially built ship called the *Roosevelt*.
- Ⓒ The Academy of Natural Sciences put Peary in charge of an expedition.
- Ⓓ Members of Peary's team turned back because of low supplies.

GO ON ▶

Harcourt • Reading and Language Skills Assessment

COMPREHENSION (continued)

Recently doctors have become worried about a health problem that can harm young people's bones. The problem is called *osteoporosis*. It can cause a person's bones to become weak and brittle. This problem often affects older people, but it rarely bothered younger people in the past.

There is a very simple way to prevent osteoporosis. All young people need to do is get enough calcium in their diets. Calcium is found in many different foods, including milk, oranges, and green vegetables.

Why has this problem suddenly started showing up in some younger people when it almost never did before? The answer probably has to do with changes in lifestyle. Most youngsters used to drink a lot of milk, and they did not eat too much junk food. Sweet drinks such as soda pop may be a big part of the problem. If a youngster has too many soda drinks, he or she probably is not drinking enough milk. Also, soda drinks contain chemicals that seem to take calcium from the bones.

13. Based on this passage, you could conclude that young people should _____.
    - (A) eat less
    - (B) drink plenty of milk
    - (C) eat sweet foods
    - (D) avoid green vegetables

14. According to this passage, there has been a change in _____.
    - (A) the way to prevent this problem
    - (B) the age group affected by this problem
    - (C) the things that cause this problem
    - (D) the way doctors treat people with this problem

STOP

Score _____

Distant Voyages / Mid-Year Skills

Harcourt • Reading and Language Skills Assessment

LITERARY RESPONSE AND ANALYSIS

Directions: Read each passage. Fill in the answer circle in front of the correct answer for each question.

One warm afternoon, Janet and Melanie sat on a blanket by Town Lake. They had finished their sandwiches and were starting on a bag of chips.

"Look at that kid over there," said Melanie. "He's pretty little to be playing near the water by himself."

Janet looked. There at the edge of the lake was a little boy no more than three years old. There were lots of families picnicking on the shore, but there were no adults near the boy as he stepped into the water.

"I'm going to go get him," said Janet.

"Maybe you shouldn't," Melanie said. "I'm sure his parents are around, and they might not like it if you picked him up."

"I don't see anyone watching him," said Janet. "If he goes in any deeper, he'll be in trouble."

"I wouldn't get involved if I were you. It's not your problem," said Melanie, opening her book.

The little boy was waist-deep in the water when Janet scooped him up. She looked around. Not far away, a woman was sleeping under a tree. Next to her were a child's pail and shovel. Janet tapped the woman gently on the arm, and she woke up with a start.

"Ronnie!" she cried, seeing her dripping son in Janet's arms.

"He was in the lake," Janet said, handing the little boy over.

"He was playing right here next to me, and I must have dozed off," Ronnie's mother said. "How can I ever thank you?"

"I was glad to help," Janet said.

GO ON

Harcourt • Reading and Language Skills Assessment

LITERARY RESPONSE AND ANALYSIS (continued)

15. The hero of this story is _____.
    (A) Melanie
    (B) Ronnie's mother
    (C) Ronnie
    (D) Janet

16. The conflict of this story is best described as a disagreement about whether to _____.
    (A) have a picnic
    (B) share a bag of chips
    (C) get involved in a problem
    (D) wake a sleeping person

17. The conflict reaches its highest point when _____.
    (A) Ronnie goes into the water
    (B) Ronnie's mother wakes up
    (C) Melanie opens her book
    (D) Ronnie's mother thanks Janet

18. The conflict between Janet and Melanie is shown mainly through _____.
    (A) the looks they give each other
    (B) things they say to each other
    (C) the way they ignore each other
    (D) things they say to other people

Harcourt • Reading and Language Skills Assessment

GO ON

Distant Voyages / Mid-Year Skills

LITERARY RESPONSE AND ANALYSIS (continued)

José and Karen walked between the bookshelves of the library. They did not want to bother the other people in the library, so José and Karen were as quiet as rabbits. José was looking for his favorite book. For José, books were doorways to adventure. Karen was at the library to use the encyclopedia. The library is a place for both fun and learning.

19. Which group of words in this story is a simile?

Ⓐ want to bother

Ⓑ as quiet as rabbits

Ⓒ at the library

Ⓓ use the encyclopedia

20. The story says that for José, books "were doorways" because books _____.

Ⓐ take the reader places

Ⓑ can be used by anybody

Ⓒ can open and close

Ⓓ are difficult to use

STOP

Harcourt • Reading and Language Skills Assessment

RESEARCH AND INFORMATION SKILLS

Directions: Study the chart and graph. Then fill in the answer circle in front of the correct answer for each question.

Jane is training for the swim team. The chart and the line graph show the number of miles she swam in different months.

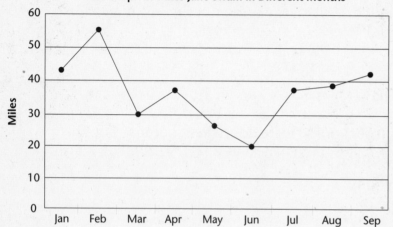

Line Graph of Miles Jane Swam in Different Months

Chart of Miles Jane Swam in Different Months	
Jan	44
Feb	56
Mar	30
Apr	37
May	27
Jun	20
Jul	37
Aug	39
Sep	42

21. What is the least number of miles Jane swam in one month?
- Ⓐ 15
- Ⓑ 20
- Ⓒ 25
- Ⓓ 30

GO ON

RESEARCH AND INFORMATION SKILLS (continued)

22. How many months does the line graph cover?

Ⓐ 9

Ⓑ 12

Ⓒ 56

Ⓓ 60

23. In which two months did Jane swim the same number of miles?

Ⓐ June, July

Ⓑ January, August

Ⓒ April, July

Ⓓ February, March

24. What is the difference between the greatest and fewest numbers of miles Jane swam?

Ⓐ 5

Ⓑ 20

Ⓒ 36

Ⓓ 76

STOP

LANGUAGE

Directions: Choose the best answer for each question.

25. Which group of words is a **sentence**?
    Ⓐ The large, shiny brass instruments.
    Ⓑ Attended the awards ceremony.
    Ⓒ Cheering loudly for the team.
    Ⓓ The crowd ran onto the field.

26. What **kind of sentence** is this?
    Hand me that hammer.
    Ⓐ declarative
    Ⓑ interrogative
    Ⓒ imperative
    Ⓓ exclamatory

27. Choose the underlined word that is the **simple subject** of this sentence.
    The photograph of the two smiling boys sat on the mantle above their grandparents' fireplace.
    Ⓐ photograph
    Ⓑ boys
    Ⓒ mantle
    Ⓓ fireplace

GO ON

LANGUAGE (continued)

Directions: Read each pair of sentences. Choose the answer that shows the best way to combine the sentences.

28. Beth went to the White House. She toured many rooms there.
    (A) Beth went to the White House and toured many rooms there.
    (B) Beth went to the White House but toured many rooms there.
    (C) Beth went to the White House or, toured many rooms there.
    (D) Beth went to the White House, but, she toured many rooms there.

29. I like most vegetables. I don't like asparagus.
    (A) I like most vegetables, or I don't like asparagus.
    (B) I like most vegetables I don't like asparagus.
    (C) I like most vegetables, but I don't like asparagus.
    (D) I like most vegetables and, I don't like asparagus.

GO ON

LANGUAGE (continued)

Directions: Choose the answer that describes the underlined words in this sentence.

30. <u>When animals walk in mud, sand, or snow</u>, their feet leave marks.
    Ⓐ coordinating conjunction
    Ⓑ dependent clause
    Ⓒ compound sentence
    Ⓓ independent clause

Directions: Choose the plural noun that is written correctly.

31. Ⓐ colonys
    Ⓑ foots
    Ⓒ oxen
    Ⓓ beachs

32. Ⓐ heros
    Ⓑ sheeps
    Ⓒ womans
    Ⓓ masses

Directions: Choose the correct possessive noun or plural noun to complete each sentence.

33. The _____ clothing department is located on the second floor.
    Ⓐ mens
    Ⓑ men's
    Ⓒ mens'
    Ⓓ mens's

34. Mark eagerly searched through the _____ of old toys in the attic.
    Ⓐ boxes
    Ⓑ boxs
    Ⓒ boxes'
    Ⓓ box's

GO ON ▶

LANGUAGE (continued)

Directions: Choose the pronoun that best completes each sentence.

35. Our aquarium is a lot of work, but it makes _____ feel happy to watch all our fish.

(A) us

(B) he

(C) we

(D) I

36. On Saturday, Jarrett helps out around _____ father's pet store.

(A) mine

(B) theirs

(C) his

(D) its

STOP

Harcourt • Reading and Language Skills Assessment

TROPHIES

Distant Voyages / Themes 1, 2, 3
Mid-Year Reading and Language Skills Assessment

Harcourt

Orlando   Boston   Dallas   Chicago   San Diego

Part No. 9997-37768-0

ISBN 0-15-332204-7 (Package of 12)

Reading and Language Skills
Assessment Pretest

Distant Voyages/Theme 4

Name _____ Date _____

SKILL AREA	Criterion Score	Pupil Score	Pupil Strength
VOCABULARY			
Word Relationships	3/4	_____	_____
Classify/Categorize	3/4	_____	_____
COMPREHENSION			
Fact and Opinion	3/4	_____	_____
LANGUAGE	7/10	_____	_____
Reflexive Pronouns			
Adjectives and Articles			
Proper Adjectives			
Comparing with Adjectives			
Main and Helping Verbs			
TOTAL SCORE	16/22	_____	

Were accommodations made in administering this test?   ☐ Yes   ☐ No

Type of accommodations: _____

_____

VOCABULARY: Word Relationships

Directions: Fill in the answer circle in front of the correct answer for each question.

1. Read the sentence.

   My mother will order clothes from the store's catalogue.

   In which sentence does the word order mean the same thing as in the sentence above?

   Ⓐ My dad's boss likes to order him around.

   Ⓑ We will order food from the lunch menu.

   Ⓒ Please arrange the words in alphabetical order.

   Ⓓ The commanding officer gave his troops an order.

2. Read the sentence.

   Be careful of the point of that stick.

   In which sentence does the word point mean the same thing as in the sentence above?

   Ⓐ The writer was trying to make a point.

   Ⓑ Please point me in the right direction.

   Ⓒ The point of your pencil should be sharp.

   Ⓓ Each question on the test is worth one point.

3. In which sentence is the underlined *homophone* used **incorrectly**?

   Ⓐ A lone wolf howled at the full moon.

   Ⓑ My parents and I went to the state fair last weekend.

   Ⓒ I got a letter from my cousin in the mail today.

   Ⓓ I have to correct all the mistakes I maid on the test.

4. In which sentence is the underlined *homophone* used **incorrectly**?

   Ⓐ The inexperienced rider was throne from his horse.

   Ⓑ The main road into town comes from the north.

   Ⓒ We must take our dog to the veterinarian today.

   Ⓓ Our neighbors let us use their pool whenever we want.

STOP

Harcourt • Reading and Language Skill Assesment

VOCABULARY: Classify/Categorize

Directions: Fill in the answer circle in front of the correct answer for each question.

5. Which word best includes the others?
   Ⓐ grain
   Ⓑ rice
   Ⓒ corn
   Ⓓ wheat

6. Which word best includes the others?
   Ⓐ circle
   Ⓑ triangle
   Ⓒ shape
   Ⓓ square

7. Which word does **not** belong?
   Ⓐ ant
   Ⓑ mosquito
   Ⓒ bee
   Ⓓ lizard

8. How are the words *tale* and *tail* related?
   Ⓐ They are synonyms.
   Ⓑ They are antonyms.
   Ⓒ They are homophones.
   Ⓓ They are homographs.

STOP

Score _____

Harcourt • Reading and Language Skill Assesment

COMPREHENSION: Fact and Opinion

Directions: Read the passage. Fill in the answer circle in front of the correct answer for each question.

Almost half the bird species in the world are songbirds. Some of them, like crows and ravens, make croaking sounds. Crows and ravens sound *terrible*! No one likes to listen to croaking sounds. Other birds make sounds that are more musical. The song of the nightingale is the most beautiful. Many poets over the years have written about nightingales. Nightingales live only in Europe. It is sad that there are no nightingales in the United States.

There are almost 4,000 different kinds of songbirds. Songbirds can perch on branches or telephone wires. Their toes grip the perch so they don't fall off. On a winter day, it's fun to see red cardinals perched on a snowy branch. They look like bright holiday decorations. Cardinals are a lot prettier than sparrows.

Most songbirds eat insects or fruit. That is why there are no songbirds in Antarctica, and very few in the desert. We are lucky to have so many song-birds in the United States. Other kinds of birds are also fascinating to study.

9. Which of these is an **opinion** from the passage?
   Ⓐ Almost half the bird species in the world are songbirds.
   Ⓑ Crows and ravens make croaking sounds.
   Ⓒ Crows and ravens sound *terrible*!
   Ⓓ Other birds make sounds that are more musical.

10. Which of these is a **fact** from the passage?
   Ⓐ No one likes to listen to croaking sounds.
   Ⓑ The song of the nightingale is the most beautiful.
   Ⓒ It is sad that there are no nightingales in the United States.
   Ⓓ Songbirds can perch on branches or telephone wires.

GO ON

COMPREHENSION: Fact and Opinion (continued)

11. Which of these is an **opinion** from the passage?
    (A) Many poets over the years have written about nightingales.
    (B) Nightingales live only in Europe.
    (C) There are almost 4,000 different kinds of songbirds.
    (D) It's fun to see cardinals perched on a snowy branch.

12. Which of these is a **fact** from the passage?
    (A) Cardinals are a lot prettier than sparrows.
    (B) Most songbirds eat insects or fruit.
    (C) We are lucky to have so many songbirds in the United States.
    (D) Other kinds of birds are also fascinating to study.

STOP

LANGUAGE

Directions: Choose the best answer for each question.

13. Which **reflexive pronoun** correctly completes this sentence?
Bryan can't forgive _____ for losing his brother's watch.

Ⓐ themselves

Ⓑ ourselves

Ⓒ himself

Ⓓ yourself

14. Which **reflexive pronoun** correctly completes this sentence?
The girls on the relay team work out daily to keep _____ in shape.

Ⓐ itself

Ⓑ herself

Ⓒ yourselves

Ⓓ themselves

Directions: Choose the underlined word in each sentence that is an **adjective**.

15. The <u>strong</u> <u>wind</u> scattered <u>clouds</u> <u>across</u> the sky.

Ⓐ strong

Ⓑ wind

Ⓒ clouds

Ⓓ across

16. The runners <u>struggled</u> to <u>catch</u> their breath as they started up the
<u>steep</u> <u>slope</u>.

Ⓐ struggled

Ⓑ catch

Ⓒ steep

Ⓓ slope

GO ON ▶

LANGUAGE (continued)

Directions: Choose the **adjective** that should be capitalized in each sentence.

17. A highpoint for <u>olympic</u> athletes occurs during the <u>opening</u> ceremony as they parade around the <u>huge</u> stadium filled with people from <u>many</u> countries.

Ⓐ olympic

Ⓑ opening

Ⓒ huge

Ⓓ many

18. The <u>spanish</u> explorer Ponce de Leon, who had sailed with Columbus on his <u>second</u> voyage, searched for the <u>fabled</u> Fountain of Youth whose waters would make <u>old</u> people young again.

Ⓐ spanish

Ⓑ second

Ⓒ fabled

Ⓓ old

Directions: Choose the form of the **adjective** that best completes each sentence.

19. The recently published novel is the _____ mystery I have ever read.

Ⓐ more suspenseful

Ⓑ most suspenseful

Ⓒ suspensefuler

Ⓓ suspensefulest

20. I think E.B. White was a _____ writer than C.S. Lewis.

Ⓐ good

Ⓑ best

Ⓒ better

Ⓓ more better

GO ON

Harcourt • Reading and Language Skill Assesment

Distant Voyages / Theme 4

LANGUAGE (continued)

Directions: Choose the **helping verb** that best completes the verb phrase.

21. Jan _____ helping me with my homework this evening.

Ⓐ can

Ⓑ is

Ⓒ do

Ⓓ has

22. Hector hopes that when he gives his report on dolphins to the class next week, his teacher _____ like it.

Ⓐ may have

Ⓑ has

Ⓒ have

Ⓓ will

STOP

· TROPHIES ·

Express Yourself / Theme 4

Reading and Language Skills Assessment

Harcourt

Orlando   Boston   Dallas   Chicago   San Diego

Part No. 9997-37765-6

ISBN 0-15-332204-7 (Package of 12)

5

· T R O P H I E S ·

Reading and Language Skills
Assessment Posttest

Distant Voyages/Theme 4

Name _____ Date _____

SKILL AREA	Criterion Score	Pupil Score	Pupil Strength
VOCABULARY			
Word Relationships	3/4	_____	_____
Classify/Categorize	3/4	_____	_____
COMPREHENSION			
Fact and Opinion	3/4	_____	_____
LANGUAGE	7/10	_____	_____
Reflexive Pronouns			
Adjectives and Articles			
Proper Adjectives			
Comparing with Adjectives			
Main and Helping Verbs			
TOTAL SCORE	16/22	_____	_____

Were accommodations made in administering this test? ❑ Yes ❑ No

Type of accommodations: _____

_____

Printed in the United States of America

ISBN 0-15-332204-7

9 10   170   10 09 08 07 06 05

VOCABULARY: Word Relationships

Directions: Fill in the answer circle in front of the correct answer for each question.

1. Read the sentence.

   Dad uses a wire brush to clean his metal tools.

   In which sentence does the word brush mean the same thing as in the sentence above?

   (A) You should brush your teeth after every meal.

   (B) The foolhardy adventurer had a close brush with disaster.

   (C) I felt the cat brush against my leg as it ran from the room.

   (D) The household cleaning product comes with a sturdy brush.

2. Read the sentence.

   I need more light to work.

   In which sentence does the word light mean the same thing as in the sentence above?

   (A) Would you please light the campfire?

   (B) There isn't enough light outside to play football.

   (C) Janell is wearing a beautiful light blue sweater.

   (D) The ballet dancer is quick and light on her feet.

3. In which sentence is the underlined *homophone* used **incorrectly**?

   (A) The stray dog is weak from lack of food.

   (B) Were you able to here what the speaker said?

   (C) You should write each answer in the space provided.

   (D) Latrelle is going to try out for the soccer team, too.

4. In which sentence is the underlined *homophone* used **incorrectly**?

   (A) The valuable painting is on lone from another museum.

   (B) The trail riders rode from dawn until dusk.

   (C) The moon shone like silver on the still surface of the sea.

   (D) My parents will pick us up in two hours.

STOP

VOCABULARY: Classify/Categorize

Directions: Fill in the answer circle in front of the correct answer for each question.

5. Which word best includes the others?
   Ⓐ pine
   Ⓑ elm
   Ⓒ tree
   Ⓓ oak

6. Which word best includes the others?
   Ⓐ sorrow
   Ⓑ emotion
   Ⓒ joy
   Ⓓ fear

7. Which word does **not** belong?
   Ⓐ concrete
   Ⓑ tin
   Ⓒ iron
   Ⓓ copper

8. How are the words *mourn* and *celebrate* related?
   Ⓐ They are synonyms.
   Ⓑ They are antonyms.
   Ⓒ They are homophones.
   Ⓓ They are homographs.

STOP

COMPREHENSION: Fact and Opinion

Directions: Read the passage. Fill in the answer circle in front of the correct answer for each question.

Some people say that you can't compare apples and oranges, but that's not true. Comparing apples with oranges is easy! First, look at their color. Oranges come in only the color orange. *Nobody* likes the color orange! Apples, on the other hand, come in many beautiful, eye-pleasing shades. There are green apples and yellow apples, red apples and yellowish-red apples. There are deep red apples and light red apples. To sum it up, *everyone* loves the colors of apples.

There are also different kinds of apples on grocery store shelves. You can buy red Delicious, golden Delicious, Jonathan, Granny Smith, Winesap, or several other kinds of apples. Red Delicious apples taste best. In the grocery stores in my town, oranges usually come in just two varieties: seedless or seeded.

Next, let's compare ease of eating. An orange has an ugly, thick rind on the outside. You have to peel off the rind to get to the part you eat. That's too much work to do just to get a bite of fruit. Apples, by contrast, can be eaten without being peeled. You can just bite right in.

Oranges and apples are similar in some ways. Both fruits were brought to this country from Europe. Apples were brought to us from England, and oranges were brought from Spain and Portugal. Both fruits can be sweet and juicy, and both fruits can be used to make juice. It is clear from the comparison done here, though, that apples are better than oranges in every way.

9. Which of these is an **opinion** from the passage?
   Ⓐ There are different kinds of apples on grocery store shelves.
   Ⓑ Red Delicious apples taste best.
   Ⓒ In my town, oranges usually come in two varieties: seedless or seeded.
   Ⓓ There are deep red apples and light red apples.

GO ON

COMPREHENSION: Fact and Opinion (continued)

10. Which of these is a **fact** from the passage?

Ⓐ Comparing apples with oranges is easy!

Ⓑ *Nobody* likes the color orange!

Ⓒ An orange has an ugly, thick rind on the outside.

Ⓓ Apples can be eaten without being peeled.

11. Which of these is an **opinion** from the passage?

Ⓐ *Everyone* loves the colors of apples.

Ⓑ You can buy Jonathan, Winesap, or other kinds of apples.

Ⓒ Both fruits can be used to make juice.

Ⓓ Both fruits were brought to this country from Europe.

12. Which of these is a **fact** from the passage?

Ⓐ Apples come in beautiful, eye-pleasing shades.

Ⓑ That's too much work to do to get a bite of fruit.

Ⓒ Apples were brought to us from England.

Ⓓ Apples are better than oranges in every way.

STOP

Score _____

Harcourt • Reading and Language Skills Assessment

LANGUAGE

Directions: Choose the best answer for each question.

13. Which **reflexive pronoun** correctly completes this sentence?
When riding in a car, you must always wear your seatbelt to protect
_____ in case an accident occurs.
  (A) themselves
  (B) yourself
  (C) itself
  (D) myself

14. Which **reflexive pronoun** correctly completes this sentence?
The copying machine will turn _____ off to save energy.
  (A) itself
  (B) himself
  (C) ourselves
  (D) herself

Directions: Choose the underlined word in each sentence that is an **adjective**.

15. Jana <u>put</u> on <u>comfortable</u> <u>shoes</u> for the hike through the <u>park</u>.
  (A) put
  (B) comfortable
  (C) shoes
  (D) park

16. Trees <u>towered</u> above the <u>floor</u> of the <u>tropical</u> <u>forest</u>.
  (A) towered
  (B) floor
  (C) tropical
  (D) forest

GO ON

LANGUAGE (continued)

Directions: Choose the **adjective** that should be capitalized in each sentence.

17. The museum in our <u>small</u> city has a <u>fine</u> collection of <u>african</u> art that attracts <u>many</u> visitors.
    - Ⓐ small
    - Ⓑ fine
    - Ⓒ african
    - Ⓓ many

18. In 1585, Sir Walter Raleigh founded England's <u>first</u> colony on the <u>north american</u> continent, but the colony failed because the settlers were <u>unprepared</u> and did not know how to survive in their <u>new</u> environment.
    - Ⓐ first
    - Ⓑ north american
    - Ⓒ unprepared
    - Ⓓ new

Directions: Choose the form of the **adjective** that best completes each sentence.

19. I am feeling _____ today than I felt yesterday.
    - Ⓐ badder
    - Ⓑ worse
    - Ⓒ most bad
    - Ⓓ worser

20. Some people feel that football is a _____ game to watch than baseball.
    - Ⓐ more exciting
    - Ⓑ most exciting
    - Ⓒ more excitinger
    - Ⓓ most excite

GO ON ➤

Distant Voyages / Theme 4

LANGUAGE (continued)

Directions: Choose the **helping verb** that best completes the verb phrase.

21. After lunch, we _____ hike to the top of the mountain.
    Ⓐ had
    Ⓑ is
    Ⓒ am
    Ⓓ will

22. I _____ assembled all the materials I need to make my model volcano.
    Ⓐ am
    Ⓑ is
    Ⓒ have
    Ⓓ do

STOP

Express Yourself / Theme 4
Reading and Language Skills Assessment

✶Harcourt

Orlando   Boston   Dallas   Chicago   San Diego

Part No. 9997-37759-1

ISBN 0-15-332204-7 (Package of 12)

· T R O P H I E S ·

Reading and Language Skills
Assessment Pretest

Distant Voyages / Theme 5

Name _____ Date _____

SKILL AREA	Criterion Score	Pupil Score	Pupil Strength
COMPREHENSION			
Text Structure: Compare and Contrast	3/4	_____	_____
Author's Purpose and Perspective	3/4	_____	_____
LITERARY RESPONSE AND ANALYSIS			
Characterization	3/4	_____	_____
LANGUAGE			
Action and Linking Verbs Present Tense Past and Future Tenses Principal Parts of Verbs Regular and Irregular Verbs	7/10	_____	_____
TOTAL SCORE	16/22	_____	_____

Were accommodations made in administering this test? ❑ Yes ❑ No

Type of accommodations: _____

_____

Printed in the United States of America

ISBN 0-15-332204-7

9 10 170 10 09 08 07 06 05

Harcourt • Reading and Language Skills Assessment

COMPREHENSION: Text Structure: Compare and Contrast

Directions: Read the passage. Fill in the answer circle in front of the correct answer for each question.

Frogs and toads are similar to each other. Adult frogs and toads have powerful leg muscles for jumping and well-developed ears for hearing. Their sticky tongues can be flipped out quickly to catch insects. Almost all of them lay eggs that hatch into tadpoles.

There are, however, some differences between frogs and toads. Frogs have smooth, moist skin and usually live very near water. They are well known for their nighttime choruses. Frogs' hind legs are longer, and they have more webbing in their feet than toads. Insects are a major part of the frog's diet.

Toads have drier, rougher skin. They often live in loose, moist soil, which is why they are common in gardens. Some live in dry areas. They hide from both the summer heat and their enemies by digging into the dirt. Because toads feed upon insects, worms, and other animals harmful to plants, the toad has been called the "gardener's friend."

1. One way in which toads and frogs are alike is that they both _____.
   - Ⓐ have strong leg muscles
   - Ⓑ hide by digging into the dirt
   - Ⓒ live very near water
   - Ⓓ are called the "gardener's friend"

2. Frogs are different from toads because toads _____.
   - Ⓐ develop from tadpoles
   - Ⓑ have sticky tongues
   - Ⓒ can live in dry areas
   - Ⓓ sing at night

GO ON

COMPREHENSION: Text Structure: Compare and Contrast (continued)

3. You can tell a frog from a toad by observing its _____.
   Ⓐ ears
   Ⓑ eggs
   Ⓒ tongue
   Ⓓ skin

4. According to this passage, both frogs and toads like to eat _____.
   Ⓐ worms
   Ⓑ insects
   Ⓒ plants
   Ⓓ soil

STOP

Harcourt • Reading and Language Skills Assessment

COMPREHENSION: Author's Purpose and Perspective

Directions: Read each passage. Fill in the answer circle in front of the correct answer for each question.

AUTHOR 1

On Tuesday, April 17, at 3:30 P.M., Mrs. Flora White drove her 1989 Chevrolet sedan into the Quick-Shine Automatic Car Wash, located at 10724 Elm Avenue. Mrs. White's twenty-year-old daughter, Maddie, was a passenger in the car. Mrs. White selected the wash-and-dry service at the ticket machine. She did not request or pay for a hot wax treatment. When a light indicated that she should proceed, Mrs. White drove her vehicle into the grooved tracks, stopping when a signal showed that she had reached the stopping point. At that time, with Mrs. White and her daughter sitting inside the vehicle with all windows closed, the car-wash mechanism mal-functioned and showered the car with hot wax. The hot-wax shower continued for approximately one-half hour, at which time another customer, Mr. D. Olson, recognized the problem and asked the attendant to turn off the machine. Both passengers in the vehicle were unharmed.

GO ON

COMPREHENSION: Author's Purpose and Perspective (continued)

AUTHOR 2

Have I got a story for you! You won't believe what happened to Flora White and Maddie when they went for a car wash at the Quick-Shine today! They were rushing to get to the Garden Club luncheon, and they zipped into the car wash for a quick rinse off. Well, when they got into position, the crazy car-wash machine went haywire! It started spraying gobs of hot wax all over the car, with Flora and Maddie trapped inside! Maddie panicked and started screaming. That frightened Flora so badly that she started squealing, too. They might've been stuck getting that hot-wax treatment all day if Mr. Olson hadn't shown up and rescued them. When Mr. Olson saw Flora and Maddie, all red in the face, wiggling frantically and waving their arms in distress, he calmly went inside and asked the attendant to come out and turn the machine off. Maddie and Flora weren't really hurt, but they were extremely upset. In fact, Flora said she felt they were almost in shock. They both went home to put ice packs on their heads and have soothing glasses of cold lemonade. Needless to say, they missed the luncheon altogether.

Harcourt • Reading and Language Skills Assessment

GO ON

COMPREHENSION: Author's Purpose and Perspective (continued)

5. The main purpose of Author 1 is to _____.
- Ⓐ persuade
- Ⓑ inform
- Ⓒ entertain
- Ⓓ warn

6. Which of the following statements would most likely be used by Author 1?
- Ⓐ The car wash has been at this location for exactly seven years.
- Ⓑ Maddie screamed, "Goodness!" and Flora screamed, "Oh, my!"
- Ⓒ The ladies scrambled out of that car like it was a house on fire!
- Ⓓ Mr. Olson had his hands full trying to deal with the two screaming women.

7. The main purpose of Author 2 is to _____.
- Ⓐ persuade
- Ⓑ inform
- Ⓒ entertain
- Ⓓ warn

8. Which of the following statements would most likely be used by Author 2?
- Ⓐ The owner of the facility could not be reached for comment as of 4:00 P.M.
- Ⓑ The car wash is fully insured by All-Safe in case of harm to vehicles.
- Ⓒ They were whooping and hollering so loudly, you'd think they were dying.
- Ⓓ Mr. D. Olson agreed to file a report at the station.

STOP

Harcourt • Reading and Language Skills Assessment

LITERARY RESPONSE AND ANALYSIS: Characterization

Directions: Read the passage. Fill in the answer circle in front of the correct answer for each question.

The water in the area was rising quickly. Brad and his father had to act fast. Who would've thought the river would overflow its banks and reach their house, a full mile or more away? There had not been a flood this bad here in more than 100 years.

"We have only a short time before the water hits us and we're stranded," Dad warned Brad. "Grab what you need and head for the car—fast! I'm not kidding around here, son. This is getting to be a life-and-death situation!"

"I understand. I'll hurry. Is there anything I can do to help you?" Brad responded.

"Just take care of getting your own things. I'll do whatever else needs to be done. Now, let's move!" Dad commanded.

Brad rushed up the stairs to his room to grab a few things. His mind was racing. He knew he'd better do exactly as his father said.

9. What can you tell about Dad from his words and actions in this story?
   (A) He can't think clearly when he is frightened.
   (B) He is hesitant to make tough decisions.
   (C) He is able to take control during a bad situation.
   (D) He is relaxed and has a good sense of humor.

10. Brad can best be described as _____.
   (A) tricky
   (B) obedient
   (C) funny
   (D) lazy

GO ON

Harcourt • Reading and Language Skills Assessment

LITERARY RESPONSE AND ANALYSIS: Characterization (continued)

11. Why does Dad say, "I'm not kidding around here, son"?
- Ⓐ to make Brad move quickly
- Ⓑ to calm Brad down
- Ⓒ to make Brad laugh
- Ⓓ to hurt Brad's feelings

12. Brad and his dad are most likely feeling _____.
- Ⓐ amused
- Ⓑ lucky
- Ⓒ alarmed
- Ⓓ jealous

STOP

LANGUAGE

Directions: Fill in the answer circle in front of the correct answer for each question.

13. Which answer correctly describes the underlined word in this sentence?

    The batter hit the <u>ball</u>, and you could hear a loud crack.

    Ⓐ action verb

    Ⓑ linking verb

    Ⓒ direct object

    Ⓓ form of verb *be*

14. The linking verb is underlined in this sentence. Which word is connected to the subject by the linking verb?

    The tourists <u>looked</u> tired as they boarded the bus that would take them to their hotel for the night.

    Ⓐ tired

    Ⓑ bus

    Ⓒ hotel

    Ⓓ night

Directions: Choose the correct verb form or verb tense to complete each sentence.

15. Robert Byrd _____ the first man to fly over both the North Pole and the South Pole.

    Ⓐ be

    Ⓑ were

    Ⓒ was

    Ⓓ am

16. The boy _____ silently as the deer nibbles at the dry grass.

    Ⓐ watch

    Ⓑ watches

    Ⓒ wachies

    Ⓓ watchs

GO ON ▶

Distant Voyages / Theme 5

LANGUAGE (continued)

17. A scientist _____ animals into kingdoms, orders, and families.

Ⓐ have classify

Ⓑ classifies

Ⓒ classifyed

Ⓓ classify

18. Yesterday morning, the climbers _____ their long trip up the mountain.

Ⓐ began

Ⓑ begun

Ⓒ has begun

Ⓓ will begin

19. When winter comes, the animals _____ to warmer regions.

Ⓐ are migrate

Ⓑ is migrating

Ⓒ has migrated

Ⓓ will migrate

20. We _____ an interesting video about ancient Egypt in class yesterday.

Ⓐ seen

Ⓑ saw

Ⓒ will see

Ⓓ do see

LANGUAGE (continued)

Directions: Look at the underlined verb or verb phrase in each sentence. Choose the answer that best describes the form of the verb.

21. Our family <u>has lived</u> in many places throughout the United States.
    Ⓐ present
    Ⓑ present participle
    Ⓒ past
    Ⓓ past participle

22. Marta <u>is collecting</u> insects for her brother's science project.
    Ⓐ present
    Ⓑ present participle
    Ⓒ past
    Ⓓ past participle

STOP

Score _____

Harcourt • Reading and Language Skills Assessment

School Rules / Theme 5
Reading and Language Skills Assessment

Harcourt

Orlando   Boston   Dallas   Chicago   San Diego

Part No. 9997-37766-4

ISBN 0-15-332204-7 (Package of 12)

5

TROPHIES

Reading and Language Skills
Assessment Posttest

Distant Voyages / Theme 5

Name _____ Date _____

SKILL AREA	Criterion Score	Pupil Score	Pupil Strength
COMPREHENSION			
Text Structure: Compare and Contrast	3/4	_____	_____
Author's Purpose and Perspective	3/4	_____	_____
LITERARY RESPONSE AND ANALYSIS			
Characterization	3/4	_____	_____
LANGUAGE			
Action and Linking Verbs	7/10	_____	_____
Present Tense			
Past and Future Tenses			
Principal Parts of Verbs			
Regular and Irregular Verbs			
TOTAL SCORE	16/22	_____	_____

Were accommodations made in administering this test?   ☐ Yes   ☐ No

Type of accommodations: _____

_____

Printed in the United States of America

ISBN 0-15-332204-7

9 10   170   10 09 08 07 06 05

COMPREHENSION: Text Structure: Compare and Contrast

Directions: Read the passage. Fill in the answer circle in front of the correct answer for each question.

I just got back from a visit to the middle school I will go to next year. It was very interesting. In middle school I will change classrooms and teachers for every subject. In my elementary school, most days we have just one teacher for science and math, and one teacher for language arts and social studies. Also, the teachers at the middle school have more special equipment for their subjects. For example, the science classroom is a laboratory with lots of work stations and sinks as well as desks and chairs.

When I go to middle school, I will have gym class every day. This year we have recess every day, but we have gym class only twice a week when the gym teacher is at our school. There is also a real auditorium that is separate from the cafeteria, instead of a big "multi-purpose room," which we use this year for lunch and assemblies.

I will still have to get up at seven o'clock to catch the school bus, and our holiday schedule is exactly the same. I will also have to continue to do homework assignments and take tests. However, the middle school seems to have a lot more to offer. In addition to all the things I mentioned above, there are clubs, sports teams, and more field trips.

1. One way in which the writer's middle school and elementary school are alike is that they both have the same _____.
   - Ⓐ teachers
   - Ⓑ cafeteria
   - Ⓒ holidays
   - Ⓓ clubs

GO ON

COMPREHENSION: Text Structure: Compare and Contrast (continued)

2. One difference between the writer's middle school and elementary school is that the middle school _____.

   (A) starts earlier in the morning

   (B) gives tests

   (C) has an auditorium

   (D) gives homework assignments

3. According to the passage, the teachers at the middle school are _____ than the teachers at the elementary school.

   (A) more specialized

   (B) friendlier

   (C) younger

   (D) happier

4. Compared to the science class at the writer's elementary school, the science class at the middle school has _____.

   (A) fewer teachers

   (B) more sinks and work stations

   (C) smarter students

   (D) fewer desks and chairs

STOP

Harcourt • Reading and Language Skills Assessment

COMPREHENSION: Author's Purpose and Perspective

Directions: Read each passage. Fill in the answer circle in front of the correct answer for each question.

AUTHOR 1

Attention all Maplewood fifth-grade students: This is your big chance! You don't have to wait until next year. You can see a middle school football game this year, absolutely free! This is your opportunity to sit in the stands with the older students who will be your schoolmates next year and cheer your lungs out for the school you will attend. To make the deal even sweeter, you don't even have to ask your parents for a ride. There will be a free bus leaving from your elementary school parking lot at 6:30 P.M. What could be finer? See you at the game!

GO ON

COMPREHENSION: Author's Purpose and Perspective (continued)

AUTHOR 2

This Thursday afternoon there will be a football game between Marshall Middle School and Tucker Middle School. Every fifth grader in the district is invited to attend. The game will begin at 7:00 P.M. at the Marshall field. A bus from each elementary school will leave at 6:30 P.M. Principal Raymond Matthews of Marshall and Principal Joanne Fine of Tucker encourage fifth graders and their parents to attend. There will be no charge for tickets, which normally cost $1.00 for students and $2.00 for parents. As Principal Fine explained, "This is a chance for the fifth graders and their parents to see a middle school football game. We hope they will come to the game."

GO ON

COMPREHENSION: Author's Purpose and Perspective (continued)

5. The main purpose of Author 1 is to _____.

Ⓐ persuade

Ⓑ inform

Ⓒ entertain

Ⓓ warn

6. Which of the following statements would most likely be used by Author 1?

Ⓐ Football games are the perfect place to show your school spirit.

Ⓑ The Tucker team is coached by American History teacher Ed Wallace.

Ⓒ Principal Matthews may consider inviting fifth graders again next year.

Ⓓ Students in other grades will have to pay the usual ticket prices.

7. The main purpose of Author 2 is to _____.

Ⓐ persuade

Ⓑ inform

Ⓒ entertain

Ⓓ warn

8. Which of the following statements would most likely be used by Author 2?

Ⓐ Look for the Marshall team to use its tremendous running game.

Ⓑ At the game, you'll feel like you're already in middle school!

Ⓒ Who could ask for a more exciting way to spend a Thursday evening?

Ⓓ Buses will return to the elementary schools when the game ends.

STOP

LITERARY RESPONSE AND ANALYSIS: Characterization

Directions: Read the passage. Fill in the answer circle in front of the correct answer for each question.

"Anne!" Coach Crawford said harshly. "Haven't you been watching the game? You're up!" Anne sat at on the bench, her mind far away. In the distance, she thought she had heard someone call her name. But she was thinking up characters for a story she wanted to write. The story would be set in olden days, like *Little House on the Prairie*, her favorite book.

"Anne!" This time it was her friend Leann, who grabbed Anne by the arm and pulled her off the bench. "Everybody's waiting for you! It's your turn at bat!"

Suddenly Anne remembered where she was. Her friends had talked her into joining their softball team. They all seemed to enjoy it, so Anne had said she would try. But here she was, bat in hand, with the ball speeding toward her. She did not think it was fun to try to hit the ball. She was not very fast, either. Even if she did get a hit, she would probably be tagged out trying to get to first base.

Anne did not want to let her team down, so she swung at the ball as hard as she could. Strike one! The pitcher threw again. Strike two! Strike three! Anne dropped the bat and trotted back to the bench. Different people like different things, she told herself. Not everyone has to like softball. She was sorry she had struck out, but as soon as she sat down, she began to think about her story again.

9. What can you tell about Anne from her words and actions in this story?

Ⓐ She is a good athlete.

Ⓑ She is interested in writing.

Ⓒ She is like Coach Crawford.

Ⓓ She very much wants to win the game.

GO ON ▶

LITERARY RESPONSE AND ANALYSIS: Characterization (continued)

10. At the beginning of the story, Coach Crawford can best be described as _____.

Ⓐ friendly

Ⓑ thoughtful

Ⓒ impatient

Ⓓ foolish

11. Why does Leann tell Anne, "Everybody's waiting for you"?

Ⓐ She wants Anne to take her turn at bat.

Ⓑ She wants to make Anne feel special.

Ⓒ She is trying to trick Anne.

Ⓓ She wants Anne to be her friend.

12. How did Anne feel at the end of the story?

Ⓐ She was terribly ashamed.

Ⓑ She was very proud of herself.

Ⓒ She was determined to do better next time.

Ⓓ She was disappointed but got over it.

STOP

LANGUAGE

Directions: Fill in the answer circle in front of the correct answer for each question.

13. Which answer correctly describes the underlined word in this sentence?

The construction worker <u>pounded</u> the nails into the hard lumber.

(A) action verb

(B) linking verb

(C) direct object

(D) form of verb *be*

14. The linking verb is underlined in this sentence. Which word is connected to the subject by the linking verb?

A biologist <u>is</u> a scientist who studies the structure of plants and animals.

(A) scientist

(B) structure

(C) plants

(D) animals

Directions: Choose the correct verb form or verb tense to complete each sentence.

15. My sister _____ thrilled that she will graduate from college tomorrow night.

(A) be

(B) is

(C) was

(D) are

16. The nurse carefully _____ the medicine to the patient's arm.

(A) applyies

(B) applyes

(C) apply

(D) applies

GO ON

Harcourt • Reading and Language Skills Assessment

LANGUAGE (continued)

17. In yesterday's experiment, the students _____ objects of different weights to see how quickly they would fall.

Ⓐ will drop

Ⓑ droped

Ⓒ dropped

Ⓓ drop

18. Over several years, the test pilot _____ many experimental aircraft.

Ⓐ fly

Ⓑ are flying

Ⓒ has flew

Ⓓ has flown

19. After two days of heavy rainfall, the river _____ to overflow its banks.

Ⓐ begin

Ⓑ began

Ⓒ begun

Ⓓ are beginning

20. When my best friend moves away, we _____ letters to each other each week.

Ⓐ will write

Ⓑ written

Ⓒ has written

Ⓓ wrote

GO ON

LANGUAGE (continued)

Directions: Look at the underlined verb or verb phrase in each sentence. Choose the answer that best describes the form of the verb.

21. We greatly <u>enjoyed</u> our trip to Yellowstone National Park.
    Ⓐ present
    Ⓑ present participle
    Ⓒ past
    Ⓓ past participle

22. By afternoon, the hikers <u>had ventured</u> deep into the forest.
    Ⓐ present
    Ⓑ present participle
    Ⓒ past
    Ⓓ past participle

STOP

Score _____

Harcourt • Reading and Language Skills Assessment

School Rules / Theme 5

Reading and Language Skills Assessment

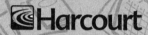

Orlando   Boston   Dallas   Chicago   San Diego

Part No. 9997-37760-5

ISBN 0-15-332204-7 (Package of 12)

5

TROPHIES

Reading and Language Skills
Assessment Pretest

Distant Voyages/Theme 6

Name _____ Date _____

SKILL AREA	Criterion Score	Pupil Score	Pupil Strength
VOCABULARY Connotation/Denotation	3/4	_____	_____
COMPREHENSION Text Structure: Cause and Effect	3/4	_____	_____
RESEARCH AND **INFORMATION SKILLS** References and Resources	3/4	_____	_____
LANGUAGE Perfect Tenses Contractions and Negatives Adverbs Comparing with Adverbs Prepositional Phrases	7/10	_____	_____
TOTAL SCORE	16/22	_____	_____

Were accommodations made in administering this test? ❑ Yes ❑ No

Type of accommodations: _____

_____

Printed in the United States of America

ISBN 0-15-332204-7

9 10 170   10 09 08 07 06 05

VOCABULARY: Connotation/Denotation

Directions: Fill in the answer circle in front of the correct answer for each question.

1. In which sentence does the underlined word have the most positive connotation?
   - Ⓐ Susan is a <u>talented</u> piano player.
   - Ⓑ Susan is a <u>good</u> piano player.
   - Ⓒ Susan is an <u>able</u> piano player.
   - Ⓓ Susan is a <u>brilliant</u> piano player.

2. In which sentence does the underlined word have the most positive connotation?
   - Ⓐ Mr. Tanaka's new car is <u>suitable</u>.
   - Ⓑ Mr. Tanaka's new car is <u>luxurious</u>.
   - Ⓒ Mr. Tanaka's new car is <u>comfortable</u>.
   - Ⓓ Mr. Tanaka's new car is <u>nice</u>.

3. In which sentence does the underlined word have the most negative connotation?
   - Ⓐ Last night's dinner was <u>unappetizing</u>.
   - Ⓑ Last night's dinner was <u>plain</u>.
   - Ⓒ Last night's dinner was <u>disgusting</u>.
   - Ⓓ Last night's dinner was <u>simple</u>.

4. In which sentence does the underlined word have the most negative connotation?
   - Ⓐ The house is filled with an <u>aroma</u>.
   - Ⓑ The house is filled with a <u>smell</u>.
   - Ⓒ The house is filled with a <u>scent</u>.
   - Ⓓ The house is filled with a <u>stench</u>.

STOP

Harcourt • Reading and Language Skills Assessment

COMPREHENSION: Text Structure: Cause and Effect

Directions: Fill in the answer circle in front of the correct answer for each question.

Water is necessary for life and is constantly being recycled in the water cycle. The energy from the sun causes water from lakes, rivers, streams, oceans, and plants to become a gas and move into the atmosphere. As the gas form of water rises in the atmosphere, it cools and turns back into liquid water as tiny droplets, forming clouds. Cloud droplets get larger by joining with other droplets. When the water droplets become too heavy to stay in the cloud, they return to the earth's surface as rain. If air temperatures are cold enough, water can fall as snow, sleet, or hail.

5. The energy that causes water to turn into a gas comes from _____.
   Ⓐ droplets
   Ⓑ clouds
   Ⓒ the sun
   Ⓓ the ocean

6. Why does the gas form of water turn back into a liquid as it rises?
   Ⓐ It cools.
   Ⓑ It hits clouds.
   Ⓒ It gets heavier.
   Ⓓ It gains energy.

GO ON ▶

COMPREHENSION: Text Structure: Cause and Effect (continued)

7. Why do water droplets fall from clouds as rain?
   - (A) The clouds explode.
   - (B) The droplets become too big.
   - (C) The sun makes them fall.
   - (D) The wind pushes them.

8. When would you expect sleet to fall instead of rain?
   - (A) When the oceans are frozen.
   - (B) When air temperatures are very cold.
   - (C) When water droplets hit each other.
   - (D) When clouds are close to the ground.

STOP

RESEARCH AND INFORMATION SKILLS: References and Resources

Directions: Read each question below. Fill in the answer circle in front of the best reference source for answering each question.

9. Which countries share a common border with France?
   Ⓐ glossary
   Ⓑ thesaurus
   Ⓒ atlas
   Ⓓ dictionary

10. Where would you look to find information for a report on global warming?
   Ⓐ dictionary
   Ⓑ online search engine
   Ⓒ atlas
   Ⓓ thesaurus

11. What are the natural resources of Thailand?
   Ⓐ print encyclopedia
   Ⓑ map
   Ⓒ globe
   Ⓓ dictionary

12. How many different meanings are there for the word *knot*?
   Ⓐ CD-ROM encyclopedia
   Ⓑ almanac
   Ⓒ atlas
   Ⓓ dictionary

STOP

Score _____

Harcourt • Reading and Language Skills Assessment

LANGUAGE

Directions: Fill in the answer circle in front of the correct answer for each question.

13. Which **verb** best completes this sentence?
By this time tomorrow, our relatives _____ for their two-week visit.
Ⓐ will have arrived
Ⓑ have arrived
Ⓒ arrived
Ⓓ arrive

14. Which **verb** best completes this sentence?
The repairmen _____ to restore electricity to the neighborhood by sundown, but they were unsuccessful.
Ⓐ will hope
Ⓑ hope
Ⓒ had hoped
Ⓓ have hoped

15. Which is the correct **contraction** to replace the underlined words in this sentence?
You had better finish mowing the yard before it begins to rain.
Ⓐ You've
Ⓑ You'll
Ⓒ You're
Ⓓ You'd

16. Which sentence does **not** contain a double negative?
Ⓐ The senator said that he wouldn't never vote for the bill.
Ⓑ Not none of the job applicants had any real work experience.
Ⓒ Some folk artists have had no formal art training.
Ⓓ I hardly never see my older brother, who is away at college.

GO ON ▶

LANGUAGE (continued)

17. Choose the underlined word that is an **adverb** in this sentence.

The alarm clock rang loudly for a long time.

Ⓐ alarm

Ⓑ loudly

Ⓒ long

Ⓓ time

18. Choose the underlined word that is an **adverb** in this sentence.

The rapids in this part of the river are quite dangerous for inexperienced canoeists.

Ⓐ rapids

Ⓑ part

Ⓒ quite

Ⓓ dangerous

19. Choose the form of the **adverb** that correctly completes this sentence.

The team played _____ because several key players were injured.

Ⓐ bad

Ⓑ worst

Ⓒ badly

Ⓓ worser

20. Choose the form of the **adverb** that correctly completes this sentence.

Because Angela has taken diving lessons, she dives _____ than I do.

Ⓐ more gracefully

Ⓑ graceful

Ⓒ most gracefully

Ⓓ gracefuller

GO ON

LANGUAGE (continued)

21. Choose the word that is the **object** of the prepositional phrase in this sentence.
Sean pulled his heavy wool sweater over his head and stood up.

(A) heavy

(B) sweater

(C) head

(D) up

22. Choose the word that is the **object** of the prepositional phrase in this sentence.
The willow trees along the riverbank have large, twisted roots.

(A) willow

(B) riverbank

(C) large

(D) roots

STOP

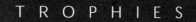

· T R O P H I E S ·

American Adventure / Theme 6
Reading and Language Skills Assessment

Harcourt

Orlando   Boston   Dallas   Chicago   San Diego

Part No. 9997-37767-2

ISBN 0-15-332204-7 (Package of 12)

5

TROPHIES

Reading and Language Skills
Assessment Posttest

Distant Voyages/Theme 6

Name _____ Date _____

SKILL AREA	Criterion Score	Pupil Score	Pupil Strength
VOCABULARY Connotation/Denotation	3/4	_____	_____
COMPREHENSION Text Structure: Cause and Effect	3/4	_____	_____
RESEARCH AND INFORMATION SKILLS References and Resources	3/4	_____	_____
LANGUAGE Perfect Tenses Contractions and Negatives Adverbs Comparing with Adverbs Prepositional Phrases	7/10	_____	_____
TOTAL SCORE	16/22	_____	_____

Were accommodations made in administering this test?   ☐ Yes   ☐ No

Type of accommodations: _____

_____

VOCABULARY: Connotation/Denotation

Directions: Fill in the answer circle in front of the correct answer for each question.

1. In which sentence does the underlined word have the most positive connotation?
   - Ⓐ Mrs. Decosto's granddaughter is <u>pretty</u>.
   - Ⓑ Mrs. Decosto's granddaughter is <u>beautiful</u>.
   - Ⓒ Mrs. Decosto's granddaughter is <u>cute</u>.
   - Ⓓ Mrs. Decosto's granddaughter is <u>attractive</u>.

2. In which sentence does the underlined word have the most positive connotation?
   - Ⓐ I had a <u>satisfactory</u> time at the party.
   - Ⓑ I had an <u>acceptable</u> time at the party.
   - Ⓒ I had a <u>decent</u> time at the party.
   - Ⓓ I had a <u>spectacular</u> time at the party.

3. In which sentence does the underlined word have the most negative connotation?
   - Ⓐ The temperature was <u>scorching</u>.
   - Ⓑ The temperature was <u>warm</u>.
   - Ⓒ The temperature was <u>unpleasant</u>.
   - Ⓓ The temperature was <u>uncomfortable</u>.

4. In which sentence does the underlined word have the most negative connotation?
   - Ⓐ The two men had a <u>discussion</u> about who was at fault.
   - Ⓑ The two men had a <u>chat</u> about who was at fault.
   - Ⓒ The two men had an <u>argument</u> about who was at fault.
   - Ⓓ The two men had a <u>debate</u> about who was at fault.

STOP

Harcourt • Reading and Language Skills Assessment

COMPREHENSION: Text Structure: Cause and Effect

Directions: Fill in the answer circle in front of the correct answer for each question.

For his birthday, Thomas's grandmother gave him a camera. It came with a case, a roll of film, and an instruction book. Thomas wanted to begin taking pictures immediately. He put the film into the camera and snapped three photos of his dog. He took a picture of each room in the house, even the attic.

His older brother was washing the car, and Thomas took his picture, too. In ten minutes Thomas had shot an entire roll of film. He asked his brother to drive him to the store, where there was a one-hour photo lab. He could hardly wait to see his pictures! Maybe he could enter them in the photography contest at school.

An hour later, Thomas's brother drove him back to the store. "I'm sorry," the man behind the counter said. "None of these photographs came out."

"That's too bad, Thomas," said his brother. "Maybe there's something wrong with the camera."

"I don't think the problem is with the camera," Thomas said. "I probably made some kind of mistake." He was disappointed, but he knew just what to do. When he got home, he read the instruction book from cover to cover. Then he reread the section about loading film. He loaded the second roll of film in his new camera and began shooting. This time he was sure he would have more success.

5. How did Thomas get a camera?
   Ⓐ His brother gave it to him.
   Ⓑ It was a birthday present.
   Ⓒ He found it in the attic.
   Ⓓ A teacher gave it to him.

GO ON

COMPREHENSION: Text Structure: Cause and Effect (continued)

6. Why did the man at the store tell Thomas that he was sorry?

Ⓐ None of the pictures came out.

Ⓑ The camera could not be repaired.

Ⓒ The store had run out of film.

Ⓓ The store no longer developed film.

7. What caused Thomas to think he had probably made a mistake?

Ⓐ The man at the store told him so.

Ⓑ He knew he hadn't read the instructions.

Ⓒ His brother told him so.

Ⓓ No other explanation was possible.

8. Thomas probably made a mistake when he _____.

Ⓐ focused the camera

Ⓑ put in the flashbulb

Ⓒ loaded the first roll of film

Ⓓ clicked the button to take the pictures

STOP

RESEARCH AND INFORMATION SKILLS: References and Resources

Directions: Read each question below. Fill in the answer circle in front of the best reference source for answering each question.

9. In what year was the Smithsonian Institution founded?
   - Ⓐ online search engine
   - Ⓑ online dictionary
   - Ⓒ online atlas
   - Ⓓ glossary

10. What is the definition of the word *tumult*?
   - Ⓐ atlas
   - Ⓑ almanac
   - Ⓒ dictionary
   - Ⓓ online encyclopedia

11. What body of water separates England from mainland Europe?
   - Ⓐ glossary
   - Ⓑ atlas
   - Ⓒ dictionary
   - Ⓓ thesaurus

12. Where could you find a synonym for the word *warm*?
   - Ⓐ online atlas
   - Ⓑ thesaurus
   - Ⓒ volume *W* of an encyclopedia
   - Ⓓ globe

STOP

Score _____

Distant Voyages / Theme 6

Harcourt • Reading and Language Skills Assessment

LANGUAGE

Directions: Fill in the answer circle in front of the correct answer for each question.

13. Which **verb** best completes this sentence?
    By 8 P.M. last evening, the hurricane _____ back out to sea.
    Ⓐ moves
    Ⓑ had moved
    Ⓒ has moved
    Ⓓ move

14. Which **verb** best completes this sentence?
    Finally, after months of searching, the scientists _____ the tomb of the ancient king.
    Ⓐ have located
    Ⓑ will have located
    Ⓒ locate
    Ⓓ will locate

15. Which is the correct **contraction** to replace the underlined words in this sentence?
    <u>We will</u> soon have enough money to make a generous donation to the wild animal orphanage.
    Ⓐ We've
    Ⓑ We'll
    Ⓒ We'd
    Ⓓ We've

16. Which sentence does **not** contain a double negative?
    Ⓐ Our society shouldn't never waste our natural resources.
    Ⓑ Not none of the executives dared oppose their boss's plan.
    Ⓒ The museum guide told us not never to touch the priceless paintings.
    Ⓓ No artist is more gifted than the young Russian pianist we heard last night.

GO ON

LANGUAGE (continued)

17. Choose the underlined word that is an **adverb** in this sentence.
    The excited students will begin their summer vacation tomorrow.
    - Ⓐ excited
    - Ⓑ begin
    - Ⓒ vacation
    - Ⓓ tomorrow

18. Choose the underlined word that is an **adverb** in this sentence.
    The newborn pups whimpered as I gently stroked their soft fur.
    - Ⓐ newborn
    - Ⓑ gently
    - Ⓒ soft
    - Ⓓ fur

19. Choose the form of the **adverb** that correctly completes this sentence.
    As our team sank the winning basket, no one jumped to his or her feet
    _____ than I did.
    - Ⓐ more quicker
    - Ⓑ most quickly
    - Ⓒ more quickly
    - Ⓓ quickest

20. Choose the form of the **adverb** that correctly completes this sentence.
    Of any of the athletes, David worked the _____ of all at improving
    his game.
    - Ⓐ more hard
    - Ⓑ hardest
    - Ⓒ most hardest
    - Ⓓ harder

GO ON

LANGUAGE (continued)

21. Choose the word that is the **object** of the prepositional phrase in this sentence.
The workers planted several shade trees by the fence.

Ⓐ workers

Ⓑ several

Ⓒ trees

Ⓓ fence

22. Choose the word that is the **object** of the prepositional phrase in this sentence.
The skillful fisherman lives close to his favorite river.

Ⓐ skillful

Ⓑ fisherman

Ⓒ his

Ⓓ river

STOP

TROPHIES

American Adventure / Theme 6
Reading and Language Skills Assessment

Harcourt

Orlando   Boston   Dallas   Chicago   San Diego

Part No. 9997-37761-3

ISBN 0-15-332204-7 (Package of 12)

5

• T R O P H I E S •

End-of-Year Reading and Language Skills Assessment

Distant Voyages / Themes 1–6

Name _____ Date _____

SKILL AREA	Criterion Score	Pupil Score	Comments
VOCABULARY (Items 1–8)	6/8	___/8	_____
COMPREHENSION (Items 9–22)	10/14	___/14	_____
LITERARY RESPONSE AND ANALYSIS (Items 23–26)	3/4	___/4	_____
RESEARCH AND INFORMATION SKILLS (Items 27–30)	3/4	___/4	_____
LANGUAGE (Items 31–40)	7/10	___/10	_____
TOTAL SCORE	**29/40**	___/40	_____

Were accommodations made in administering this test? ☐ Yes ☐ No

Type of accommodations: _____

_____

Printed in the United States of America

ISBN 0-15-332204-7

9 10 170 10 09 08 07 06 05

VOCABULARY

Directions: Read each sentence. Fill in the answer circle in front of the correct answer for each question.

1. **The doctor takes your temperature with a thermometer.**
   What part of the word *thermometer* means "heat"?
   Ⓐ the
   Ⓑ therm
   Ⓒ mom
   Ⓓ meter

2. Which root word means *hundred*?
   Ⓐ "scope" as in **telescope**
   Ⓑ "centi" as in **centipede**
   Ⓒ "voc" as in **vocal**
   Ⓓ "bio" as in **biology**

3. Read the sentence.

   I need to use the bicycle pump.

   In which sentence does the word pump mean the same thing as in the sentence above?
   Ⓐ The candidate made sure to pump the hands of all the guests.
   Ⓑ The policemen had to pump the witness for information.
   Ⓒ Some ranchers use a pump to get water from the ground.
   Ⓓ My mother stepped in a hole and broke the heel of her pump.

4. In which sentence is the underlined *homophone* used **incorrectly**?
   Ⓐ Hour job is to rake and bag the leaves.
   Ⓑ The Martins will soon begin their trip to Florida.
   Ⓒ Darin has saved enough money to buy a video game.
   Ⓓ We rode in a cab from the airport to the hotel.

GO ON

VOCABULARY (continued)

5. Which word best includes the others?
   Ⓐ volleyball
   Ⓑ soccer
   Ⓒ basketball
   Ⓓ sport

6. How are the words *mend* and *repair* related?
   Ⓐ They are synonyms.
   Ⓑ They are antonyms.
   Ⓒ They are homophones.
   Ⓓ They are homographs.

7. In which sentence does the underlined word have the most positive connotation?
   Ⓐ Rescuing the pet from the burning house was an <u>appropriate</u> act.
   Ⓑ Rescuing the pet from the burning house was a <u>good</u> act.
   Ⓒ Rescuing the pet from the burning house was a <u>heroic</u> act.
   Ⓓ Rescuing the pet from the burning house was a <u>respectable</u> act.

8. In which sentence does the underlined word have the most positive connotation?
   Ⓐ The audience was <u>interested</u> in the magician's performance.
   Ⓑ The audience was <u>astonished</u> by the magician's performance.
   Ⓒ The audience was <u>impressed</u> with the magician's performance.
   Ⓓ The audience was <u>accepting</u> of the magician's performance.

STOP

Score _____

Harcourt • Reading and Language Skills Assessment

COMPREHENSION

Directions: Read each passage. Fill in the answer circle in front of the correct answer for each question.

In 1993 scientists made a spectacular discovery. They were doing research in a rain forest. The rain forest was on the island of Cuba. The scientists were looking for unusual woodpeckers. What the scientists found was even more important than woodpeckers.

The scientists discovered a frog that is only about one centimeter long. It is an adorable little creature with a cute orange stripe on its black body. This was a very lucky and exciting discovery.

Some of the scientists were from Havana, Cuba. Other members of the team were from Pennsylvania State University. They discovered the frog under a pile of leaves when they heard it chirp. It makes a very strange sound.

The scientists learned some amazing things about their new discovery. For example, most frogs lay hundreds of eggs at a time, but this frog lays only one. There were other fascinating things about this unusual amphibian. Wonderful discoveries are made when scientists from different countries work together.

9. Which of these is a **fact** from the passage?
   - (A) This was a very lucky and exciting discovery.
   - (B) The scientists discovered a frog that is only about one centimeter long.
   - (C) What the scientists found was even more important than woodpeckers.
   - (D) It is an adorable little creature with a cute orange stripe on its black body.

10. Which of these is an **opinion** from the passage?
   - (A) Some of the scientists were from Havana, Cuba.
   - (B) Other members of the team were from Pennsylvania State University.
   - (C) They discovered the frog under a pile of leaves when they heard it chirp.
   - (D) It makes a very strange sound.

GO ON

COMPREHENSION (continued)

No one would have believed that Wilma Rudolph would grow up to be an Olympic athlete. Wilma, the twentieth child in a family with twenty-two children, was small and sickly from the day she was born. When she was almost five, though, Wilma became sicker than she had ever been. Her leg and foot became weak and twisted. The doctor told her family that Wilma had polio and that she would never walk again.

Even though Wilma's family was poor, her mother took her on the bus twice every week to a hospital fifty miles away. There doctors and nurses helped Wilma do exercises to strengthen her leg. She practiced the exercises faithfully, even though they were painful. In time, the doctors put a steel brace on Wilma's leg that allowed her to walk. Wilma's mother, brothers, and sisters encouraged her to keep doing her leg exercises at home. One Sunday when Wilma was a little older, she took off her heavy leg brace and walked down the aisle at her church. After that, she practiced walking as much as she could. When she turned twelve, she took off her leg brace forever.

By the time Wilma was in high school, she had gotten so much stronger that she was a basketball star. At one game, a college coach saw her. He was impressed by the way she ran and wanted her to be on his track and field team. He helped her get a college scholarship.

In the summer of 1960, Wilma represented the United States as a runner at the Olympics in Rome. She ran better than she had ever run before. She became the first American woman to win three gold medals in track—for the 100-meter dash, the 200-meter dash, and the 400-meter relay. After once being told that she would never walk again, Wilma had become the fastest woman runner in the world.

GO ON

COMPREHENSION (continued)

11. The author's main purpose in this passage is to _____.

   Ⓐ persuade

   Ⓑ inform

   Ⓒ entertain

   Ⓓ warn

12. Which of these is an **opinion** from the passage?

   Ⓐ Wilma was the twentieth child in a family with twenty-two children.

   Ⓑ Wilma's mother took her on the bus twice a week to a hospital fifty miles away.

   Ⓒ No one would have believed that Wilma Rudolph would grow up to be an Olympic athlete.

   Ⓓ Wilma represented the United States as a runner at the Olympics in Rome.

13. What is the best summary of this passage?

   Ⓐ Wilma Rudolph had polio as a child and was told that she would never walk again. Doctors and nurses helped her do exercises to strengthen her leg, and Wilma practiced the exercises faithfully. Eventually she became so strong that she won three gold medals in track at the Olympics.

   Ⓑ Wilma Rudolph was the twentieth child in a family with twenty-two children. She was always small and sickly from the day she was born.

   Ⓒ When Wilma Rudolph was almost five, she became sicker than she had ever been. Her mother, brothers, and sisters encouraged her to do leg exercises.

   Ⓓ Wilma Rudolph was a star basketball player and a member of the 1960 U.S. Olympic team. When she competed in Rome, she won a gold medal in the 400-meter relay.

GO ON

COMPREHENSION (continued)

There are thousands of species of birds on earth. Most birds can be classed into four major groups: flightless birds, water birds, perching birds, and birds of prey.

Flightless birds cannot fly, but some are fast runners and others are strong swimmers. Flightless birds include penguins, ostriches, kiwis, and emus. Penguins have strong flight muscles, but their wings have been changed into flippers. They flap their wings to swim underwater. Ostriches can run up to forty miles per hour.

Water birds usually have webbed feet for swimming, but they can also fly. Cranes, ducks, geese, swans, pelicans, and loons are all water birds. The loon can stay underwater for several minutes while it hunts for fish. Ducks walk clumsily on land, but they are swift swimmers and excellent divers, and they can fly fast and far.

Perching birds can perch on a branch. When a perching bird lands on a branch, its feet automatically close around the branch. This keeps the bird from falling off even when it is asleep. Robins, wrens, warblers, and sparrows are all perching birds. Many perching birds are songbirds.

Birds of prey are meat eaters. Eagles, hawks, owls, and falcons are all birds of prey. They kill and eat fish, reptiles, and other animals. Their sharp, curved beaks and powerful feet with sharp claws help them catch and eat their prey. They can also see very well, which helps them hunt for food. Most birds of prey hunt during the day. Certain owls, though, hunt only at night. They can see well even in the dark, and their keen sense of hearing helps them find their prey.

Harcourt • Reading and Language Skills Assessment

GO ON

COMPREHENSION (continued)

14. One way that ducks and penguins are the same is that they are both _____.

   Ⓐ strong swimmers

   Ⓑ fast flyers

   Ⓒ meat eaters

   Ⓓ songbirds

15. One way that eagles and hawks are the same is that they both _____.

   Ⓐ can stay underwater a long time

   Ⓑ have feet that automatically close around a branch

   Ⓒ have sharp claws

   Ⓓ are flightless

16. One way that some owls are different from other birds of prey is that some owls _____.

   Ⓐ eat fish

   Ⓑ hunt only at night

   Ⓒ are songbirds

   Ⓓ have webbed feet

GO ON

Harcourt • Reading and Language Skills Assessment

COMPREHENSION (continued)

Crazy Horse, the great Oglala Sioux Indian chief who helped defeat Custer at the Battle of Little Bighorn, was born in the early 1840s. Even as a child Crazy Horse was different from other boys his age. He was small, shy, quiet, and serious, and he liked to spend time alone. His mother died when he was young, and he was raised by his mother's sister. His father loved him and played with him a lot. As a child in a Sioux village, Crazy Horse was probably pampered by all the adults in the village.

Crazy Horse was taught all the skills he needed to grow up on the plains. He learned to ride bareback, controlling his horse with his knees and leaping from one horse to another. He also learned to hunt and to fight. He practiced shooting his bow and arrows and had contests with his friends to see who could shoot the best. Although he became an expert with a bow, he was never vain or boastful about his skills. By the time he was ten or eleven, he was so good at riding and hunting that he joined the men on hunts for wild horses or buffalo.

Crazy Horse and his friends also learned the ways of nature. They learned the different kinds of birds and the calls they made; they learned the habits of the animals. They also learned to study the sky to judge the weather. They were taught that everything in nature has a lesson to teach and that each living thing is sacred.

When Crazy Horse was about thirteen, he had a powerful vision. It showed that he would never be hurt by the arrows and bullets of his enemies. From then on, he tied a small stone behind his ear, put a hawk's feather in his hair, painted a red lightning bolt on his cheek, and put dust on himself and his pony before each battle so he would look the same as he did in his vision. Believing that staying true to his vision protected him from being killed, he fought boldly in many battles.

GO ON

Distant Voyages / End-of-Year Skills

COMPREHENSION (continued)

17. What is the main idea of this passage?

   Ⓐ Crazy Horse learned to ride bareback, controlling his horse with his knees and leaping from one horse to another.

   Ⓑ Crazy Horse, growing up on the plains, learned skills in his youth that helped him to become a great Oglala Sioux Indian chief.

   Ⓒ As a child in a Sioux village, Crazy Horse was pampered by all the adults.

   Ⓓ As a boy, Crazy Horse had a powerful vision that he would not be hurt in battle.

18. The passage says that Crazy Horse was different from other boys his age because he _____.

   Ⓐ shot a bow and arrows

   Ⓑ learned different bird calls

   Ⓒ studied the sky to judge the weather

   Ⓓ was serious and liked to be alone

19. What did Crazy Horse do before each battle?

   Ⓐ bathed in ice-cold water

   Ⓑ chose a white horse to ride

   Ⓒ put a hawk's feather in his hair

   Ⓓ tied on a special necklace

20. The author thinks that Crazy Horse _____.

   Ⓐ was a skilled rider, hunter, and fighter

   Ⓑ was hotheaded and foolish

   Ⓒ should have lost at Little Bighorn

   Ⓓ did not get a good education

GO ON

COMPREHENSION (continued)

> John F. Kennedy was our thirty-fifth president. In 1960, he won a close election against Richard Nixon. Many people thought Nixon would win because he had been vice-president under Dwight Eisenhower, a popular leader. One thing that helped Kennedy was television. He was a handsome young man who came across well on TV. When he debated Nixon, many people who heard the debate on radio thought Nixon had won, but most who watched it on television thought Kennedy had won.
>
> Kennedy was a war hero. During World War II, his patrol boat was rammed by an enemy ship. Kennedy and his men swam for their lives to a nearby island. He not only swam for hours, but he did it while towing an injured crewman!
>
> As president, Kennedy faced many important challenges, such as the Cuban Missile Crisis, which was caused by the Soviet Union. For several days it seemed that a war could start at any second. Finally, the Soviets backed down.
>
> President Kennedy was the youngest man ever elected president in 1960, and he became the youngest president to die in office. The nation mourned his death.

21. What helped Kennedy win the election in 1960?
    - (A) his voice on the radio
    - (B) his appearance on television
    - (C) his experience as vice-president
    - (D) the support of Soviet leaders

22. Why did Kennedy's boat sink during World War II?
    - (A) It was struck by another ship.
    - (B) It ran aground on an island.
    - (C) It was hit by a bomb.
    - (D) It was old and full of leaks.

STOP

Harcourt • Reading and Language Skills Assessment

LITERARY RESPONSE AND ANALYSIS

Directions: Read each passage. Fill in the answer circle in front of the correct answer for each question.

Kyra was having a costume party on Saturday night. She had invited all her friends. By 7:30, almost all the guests were there. Everyone was laughing and having fun. Suddenly, Kyra's friend Derek glanced across the fence into the yard next door. He saw Carl, one of their classmates, staring over into the party group and looking pretty miserable. Carl wasn't wearing a costume, and he looked as though he felt left out.

Derek made his way over to Kyra. He said, "Kyra, I just saw Carl looking over at us. I didn't know he lived next door to you. You DID invite Carl to your party, didn't you?"

"Gosh, Derek! I'm not sure," Kyra replied. "I *meant* to ask him, but maybe I forgot. What do you think we should do now? He must feel awful seeing all of us over here and thinking he wasn't invited."

"I'll go over and talk to him," Derek said. "I'll tell him that we're all waiting for him. I'll make it sound like he *was* invited and we're wondering why he's so late."

"Oh, please do! I feel just awful that he's over there thinking I didn't invite him on purpose. Do you think you can convince him?"

"I'll do my best," Derek answered as he started walking toward Carl's house.

A few minutes later, Derek and Carl came back to the party together. Carl was laughing and smiling. He had on overalls, a red bandanna, and a straw hat.

Derek said, "Look, everyone! Farmer Carl finally showed up!"

GO ON

LITERARY RESPONSE AND ANALYSIS (continued)

23. What can you tell about Derek from his words and actions in this story?

Ⓐ He is shy about being in a large group.

Ⓑ He is kind and doesn't want anyone to have hurt feelings.

Ⓒ He always wants to be the center of attention.

Ⓓ He is tricky and likes to play jokes on other people.

24. You can tell from Kyra's words and actions that she _____.

Ⓐ is worried that Carl might feel left out

Ⓑ does not care whether Derek talks to Carl or not

Ⓒ is only interested in what people think of her costume

Ⓓ does not like Derek and wants him to leave the party

25. At the end of this story, Carl is most likely feeling _____.

Ⓐ worried

Ⓑ angry

Ⓒ cheerful

Ⓓ frightened

26. Why does Derek say, "Look, everyone! Farmer Carl finally showed up"?

Ⓐ He wants the others to make fun of Carl's costume.

Ⓑ He is afraid no one will know Carl unless he tells who he is.

Ⓒ He wants to make Carl feel guilty about arriving so late for the party.

Ⓓ He wants everyone to welcome Carl and to think he was invited all along.

STOP

Harcourt • Reading and Language Skills Assessment

RESEARCH AND INFORMATION SKILLS

Directions: Read each question below. Fill in the answer circle in front of the best reference source for answering each question.

27. What are the languages spoken in Jamaica?
    - Ⓐ atlas
    - Ⓑ thesaurus
    - Ⓒ globe
    - Ⓓ CD-ROM encyclopedia

28. What is the definition of the science term *herbivore*?
    - Ⓐ glossary
    - Ⓑ almanac
    - Ⓒ atlas
    - Ⓓ globe

29. What states border New York?
    - Ⓐ glossary
    - Ⓑ thesaurus
    - Ⓒ online atlas
    - Ⓓ dictionary

30. Where could you find information for a report on sleep disorders?
    - Ⓐ glossary
    - Ⓑ online search engine
    - Ⓒ atlas
    - Ⓓ dictionary

STOP

Harcourt • Reading and Language Skills Assessment

LANGUAGE

Directions: Fill in the answer circle in front of the correct answer for each question.

31. Choose the adjective that best completes this sentence.

The cheetah is the _____ of all animals for running short distances.

(A) most fast

(B) more fast

(C) fastest

(D) faster

32. Choose the adverb that best completes this sentence.

The frightened animal _____ disappeared into its burrow.

(A) more quick

(B) quick

(C) quickest

(D) quickly

33. Choose the adverb that best completes this sentence.

Jamie can hit the ball _____ than anyone on our softball team.

(A) farther

(B) farthest

(C) more far

(D) most farthest

Harcourt • Reading and Language Skills Assessment

GO ON

LANGUAGE (continued)

34. The linking verb is underlined in this sentence. Which word is connected to the subject by the linking verb?

The volunteers <u>appeared</u> eager to clean the empty lot by mowing the grass and picking up trash.

Ⓐ volunteers

Ⓑ eager

Ⓒ lot

Ⓓ grass

35. Choose the answer that best describes the underlined verb phrase.

The researcher <u>is gathering</u> valuable data to support the theory.

Ⓐ present

Ⓑ present participle

Ⓒ past

Ⓓ past participle

36. Choose the word that is the **object** of the prepositional phrase in this sentence.

The skillful football player kicked the ball between the goalposts to score the extra points.

Ⓐ skillful

Ⓑ player

Ⓒ ball

Ⓓ goalposts

GO ON

LANGUAGE (continued)

Directions: Choose the correct verb form or verb tense to complete each sentence.

37. In 1271, Marco Polo _____ his historic journey to China.
- Ⓐ began
- Ⓑ begun
- Ⓒ will begin
- Ⓓ will have begun

38. A geologist _____ the history of the earth by looking at rock formations.
- Ⓐ have study
- Ⓑ studys
- Ⓒ studies
- Ⓓ studyied

39. By tomorrow evening, our first snow of the season _____.
- Ⓐ fell
- Ⓑ will have fallen
- Ⓒ had fallen
- Ⓓ falls

40. By 8 P.M., I _____ my homework and was ready to watch TV.
- Ⓐ had finished
- Ⓑ am finishing
- Ⓒ finish
- Ⓓ will finish

STOP

Score _____ *Distant Voyages / End-of-Year Skills*

Harcourt • Reading and Language Skills Assessment